advance praise for MEN I HATE

"*Men I Hate* performs the surgical accomplishment of dissecting a life while enacting a delicate transition from rage and fear into empathy and understanding. D'Amico gifts readers life-sustaining insights by immersing them inside the exhilarations, frustrations, and exhaustions of being a daughter, a lesbian, a wife, a writer, a patient, a citizen, and a human. Without shying away from the complicated details of a life that demands shifts in how she defines and understands herself, she skillfully guides us through many challenges we all face. One can only have gratitude for the perspective and hope she provides as she masterfully unlearns the past in order to meet the present."

—Claudia Rankine, author of *Citizen: An American Lyric*

"With a disarming blend of candor and style, Lynette D'Amico traces the tectonic shifts of a long-term relationship with exhilarating clarity. *Men I Hate* confronts the hardest questions—what happens when everything you thought you knew changes?—and does so without flinching. An impelled, acoustically alive, unforgettable book."

—Paul Lisicky, author of *Song So Wild and Blue: A Life with the Music of Joni Mitchell*

"Lynette D'Amico gives free play to the stories within the stories, the countervailing stories, the stories that split the truth right down the middle of the stories we tell ourselves and those that we live by. Tough, insightful, purely conceived, and deeply contextualized, *Men I Hate* passionately investigates a history of desire retold, transformed, and possibly undone when one member of a lesbian couple transitions. D'Amico's deft, fresh grasp of the essay delivers us to a form that can withstand the shattering, shelter the thrown, and accommodate the contradictions, all the while moving across uncharted terrain. *Men I Hate* is a knockout."

—Mary Cappello, coauthor of *Buffalo Trace: A Threefold Vibration*

"*Men I Hate* is a book about a relationship that's really about a relationship to self—from escaping the myth of the American dream to negotiating the tyranny of gender rules and roles to facing the complications of family, romance, aging, illness, and the search for home. Here Lynette D'Amico inhabits all her insecurities—her rage, heartbreak, and longing—with rare precision so that facing grief might offer the possibility for comfort."

—Mattilda Bernstein Sycamore, author of *Terry Dactyl*

men i hate

21ST CENTURY ESSAYS
David Lazar and Patrick Madden, Series Editors

men i hate

A MEMOIR IN ESSAYS

lynette d'amico

MAD CREEK BOOKS, AN IMPRINT OF
THE OHIO STATE UNIVERSITY PRESS
COLUMBUS

Library of Congress Cataloging-in-Publication data available online at https://catalog.loc.gov
LCCN: 2025041926
Identifiers: ISBN 9780814259696 (paperback); ISBN 9780814284575 (ebook)

Cover design by Brock Book Designs
Text design by Juliet Williams
Type set in Georgia

∞ The paper used in this publication meets the minimum requirements of the American National Standard for Information Sciences—Permanence of Paper for Printed Library Materials. ANSI Z39.48-1992.

For Carl, my presence of possibility,
who makes my life livable

contents

changing the story

IN THIS PHOTO: me as a young, bushy-haired girl who dreamed of looking like a bullfighter or Bernardo in *West Side Story*: tight pants, bolero jacket, an open-necked shirt, soft black leather boots.

I knew I would be better looking as a boy. I would be a better dancer. I would be handsome, dark as mystery, the last of the Mohicans, raised by wolves. I wanted to split wood, smoke on the street, spit, and swagger. I wanted to piss standing up. I wanted free throws, double plays, home runs, girls girls girls. With a bear-sticking knife, pants with pockets, a canteen, and knapsack, I could be a boy. I could cut my hair short, run away and join the army. I wanted to walk with power and authority through all the realms of life, to sit wide-legged, a girl at my side, a soft, dewy creature who smelled of lavender and vanilla.

Wanting a girl didn't mean that I wanted to be a boy. I was a girl who liked girls, which was different from a girl who was a boy who liked girls.

IN THIS PHOTO: my husband at age six in a cowboy hat and gun and holster.

I believe objects hold history and personal memory: the brick

arch of a church entrance in Venice, my grandmother's rosary—
Jesus worn to an abstract nub on the cross—a set of twelve cocktail forks still in the box from the buffet in my parents' dining
room, a porcelain pull-chain light fixture in the basement of
the house where I lived in Minneapolis. Their history is specific—the arch of Basilica di Santa Maria Gloriosa dei Frari was
built in the fourteenth century. My grandmother was Sicilian.
She didn't speak or write English, she prayed. I use the cocktail
forks I inherited when entertaining. Small bites, small forks. I
painstakingly scraped splatters of old paint off the light fixture. I
know by the design and label that it was from the 1930s. I know
these things. I hold them in my hands. I am tourist, owner, witness, but photographs, like memory and history, are vulnerable
to interpretation. So, the photo?

Before my husband was my husband, before *he* was a *he,* he
was a small girl called P——[1] in cowboy gear.

"I was never a girl," my husband says.

In W. G. Sebald's novel *Austerlitz,* a scholar of architectural history seeks to recover or imagine his personal history, which he
has no memory of before the age of four. The main character,
whose name echoes the title of the book, keeps a collection of
old photographs on a large table, some of which appear throughout the book. Nightly, he shuffles the photographs so the images

---

1. "P——" indicates my husband's birth first name. With his permission
I refer to him as "P——" where it reflects the time/place of certain previous
moments in our relationship and experiences together, and as "Carl" in most
places throughout the book, which is what he goes by.

form new patterns and new relationships emerge to make new histories, new stories.

Two years after top surgery, starting testosterone in 2017, my husband tells me he is talking to a lawyer about changing his name. We are in the kitchen, there are orange dishes on the table. He says he will also discuss whether he is changing his gender markers too. I blurt, "You're a man now? We never talked about that." He says, "But what does *he* and *husband* mean? How does *woman* make sense to you?"

As I started writing about my response to my husband's gender transition, I considered again and again: What do I owe the people I am writing about? What is the line between my own story and my husband's? During his transition, all my friends were asking me questions, my therapist was asking me questions: "How are you feeling about your husband's gender transition? How do you make sense of your husband's transition? How has his transition changed your life? Are you still a lesbian?" Trying to sort out my own feelings, I submitted an essay—this essay—to a well-known and well-respected literary journal that sent me what felt like a scathing rejection. Every rejection feels a little scathing, but this one felt directly and personally shaming. The rejection made me stop to consider beyond my own thinking. The editor said that while my essay had generated a lot of discussion, ultimately the decision was made not to accept it because the piece had not addressed whether I had my husband's consent to write about his gender transition.

IN THIS PHOTO: my husband wearing a three-piece gray suit with a purple patterned shirt and purple tie. The suit was custom made, the tie shortened so it doesn't hang over his belt; the black wing-tip shoes are hard and shiny. He looks dapper and miniature. The unhoused chat him up on the street, children trust him on sight like he is one of their own. He is approachable, accommodating, anxious—but not masculine, not manly.

What is the meaning of this shape, this form, the gender we are born to? I have built a life on the certainty of discrete things: his smooth face, his narrow shoulders, our history, this marriage.

My husband had never talked to me about wanting to be a man—a boy, yes. A boy, as in someone able to move with fluidity through the world—quick and bold without the self-consciousness or the stigma of being a middle-aged woman. Which my husband dreaded becoming. The dread didn't originate in some kind of Peter Pan, forever-young fantasy but in the finality and wrongness of that identity. For him. Wrong for him. Not wrong for me or for other women. My husband's original intention was to live somewhere in the nonfemale nonmale in between. Which made a kind of sense to me. The limitations of the gender binary never made sense to me for anybody, for any body. Trans made sense. He'd still be himself.

In a relationship, a world is built, a history constructed story by story, image by image. I tell my husband that as a child I ran back and forth in the vacant lot at the end of the block where we lived in a suburb of St. Louis County and imagined myself a pony. He tells me he hit a tennis ball against the garage door of his childhood home in Elkhart, Indiana, until his arm was numb, past the call to come in for dinner, past dusk into darkness. I tell him I always passed, I was never queer except with a lover. He tells me he was in a car accident in Orlando a long time ago and his back sometimes still hurts.

Under the crushing weight of the erasure of all things female, I am daring to speak, to try to own, to claim. How complicit are husbands in such a world? How much falls on me, as the wife, the woman, to navigate this particular silencing? My question was: Don't I have the right to the material of my life? But stories that don't contain counterstories are ultimately false or at least incomplete. I think there are multiple stories within any "true" story. If I chose to write something that involves another person, I'd better have done the work to become aware, to have asked the questions, to have considered the consequences. Because ultimately, it's not about who has the right to write about things, places, experiences, and other people. Rather, it's about how we take consideration of others. How we treat others. How we value them as fully human.

My husband collected teddy bears, stuffed bears and Christmas ornaments, bear earrings and teddy T-shirts.

"When was this?"

"Before I knew you."

Pretransition, we were visiting my husband's parents in Indiana. Every visit is tightly dictated by my husband's father's mandates and routines. Only sports and westerns on TV, the thermostat cranked to 74, my father-in-law in the latest half-zip pullover we buy him every year, the TV remote in his hand. We are going out to dinner at Red Lobster. I watch my husband's father step off a curb, leading with his paunch, listing from side to side, leaving my mother-in-law on the sidewalk, walking ahead of his wife, daughter, and daughter-in-law. My husband takes his mother's arm. "He's always in such a hurry," his mother comments, head down.

IN THIS PHOTO: my husband in a cap and gown, holding a framed diploma; a black smear, a dog in motion, half in and half out of the frame.

It seemed to me my husband was most himself in a classroom, the smartest person in the room, or on a basketball court, stutter-step and drive, his body a wall nobody got by. He could move the ball down court, move the conversation where he wanted it to go, and he didn't mind charging anybody who got in his way. Pretransition, he couldn't order takeout on the phone, return a purchase, or make a left turn, but he could work his elbows, his arms like weapons. He could slam an intellectual opponent like dunking a ball, suspended above the basket, the world on mute. It all fit together: the ball in his hands, the ball in the basket; whip-tongue smart. For a girl. For a short, quick girl, slippery as a lie, who could talk the paint off a wall.

I'd never lived with dogs before I knew him. I thought dogs were psychically invasive. I didn't want that abandon, that open-hearted, open-mouthed intent. I believed in the quiet, self-con-tained devotion of cats, capricious, pure as murder. I love you and I might kill you. Cats were my people. Together, my husband and I have loved generations of dogs, from the jumping licking panting dog, to the messy princess who grew up in a hamlet in the Berkshires, to our dearest boy who shook during thunderstorms and on the happiest day of his life killed a whole nest of baby bunnies.

We didn't really identify as a lesbian couple. I didn't identify as lesbian—too hard-edged, too limiting, too many rules. I was femme until middle age blurred that designation. Among my femme sister-friends, who ranged from sporto femme, to woman-loving-woman femme, to bottle blonde buxom femme, I was hetero femme—*straight passing*—although the term makes me bristle. My husband was never a woman, never lesbian. Together, we were a version of a same-gender queer couple.

Chocolate or vanilla? East Coast or West Coast? Gay or straight? When I was still in the morass of sexual exploration, I got cornered at a party by a boy-girl couple who asked me repeatedly, "Chocolate or vanilla? Chocolate or vanilla?" Whatever I said—Strawberry? Butterscotch? Mint chocolate chip?—they would launch like evangelical determinists into a formulaic response about probability and free will, the intention of which was to refute my response. "Your choice is an unfolding of the given. There is no choice in your choice." And what were we talking about anyway? Ice cream? Choice? Three-ways? Is my husband's predetermination of maleness a rejection of his femaleness? An addition? Like an add-on, a portable penis, a physical and psychic remodeling.

I wonder: If I were more female, would that make him sufficiently male to appease his restless searching for a gender that works for him, that fits? Are we who we are in relation to the other?

In March of 2017, six months on testosterone, my husband calls me from a hotel in New York. He has been drinking. He is outraged, raging, heartbroken: "I wish I were a woman. I've been called *she* and *ma'am* all day—I wish I could just embrace womanhood—I would honestly do it for you, but I need my 'I' to be *me* and it's not *her*."

My husband notes every instance of misgendering: at work, out in the world, with friends, with colleagues, in daily interactions. His notice ignites one firestorm after another until we are burning, flames all around. "The waiter didn't even look at us," I say, bewildered. "You have to be patient. People who have known you for years need time to adjust."

He is introduced in a professional setting by the wrong name, the wrong pronoun. I think about a service that would scrub the internet of his old identity, that would erase our history. I think about the unreliability of memory, of history.

I call him nothing. I can't say his new name. I miss who he was. I call him nothing. I say, "Hey!" I don't notice when a waiter says, "What can I get you ladies?" I don't notice when our neighbor refers to my husband as "big sister" to their six-year-old son. I feel like I'm trying to navigate our marriage underwater. I don't notice until I turn around, look up, and my husband is pushing back his chair, incensed, "Let's get out of here," and we leave, still hungry. "Was everything okay?" the waiter asks. No, nothing is okay. Nothing will ever be okay again.

I start to anticipate occasions of misgendering, and I try to intercept them: I call the hair stylist where my husband is going to get his hair cut and tell them his preferred pronouns are "he and him." I make a reservation for dinner and ask the restaurant to make a note to ask the wait staff to use masculine pronouns.

"This is my transition!" my husband yells at me. "Stop stepping on my heels, just stop."

I wince while talking to friends who consistently misgender him. I wince when he is misgendered and the person corrects themselves. We are all tripping over pronouns. I am watchful and vigilant and so anxious that I look for distraction in the daily onslaught of inane or terrifying Trump tweets, Netflix binge watching, cooking elaborate meals that require marinating and spice mixes and complicated ingredient layering. Strain the broth into a large bowl; cool to room temperature. Chill in the refrigerator for several hours, until the fat rises to the top of the bowl and congeals. Skim off the fatty fat feminine pronouns until every syllable is stripped clear and adamant.

I feel stalked by the pronoun police. I can't read, I'm not writing. I say yes to writing solicitations and then ask for a deadline extension and then the missed deadlines pile up. I have nothing to say. I have no "I" to speak from.

If he is now a man, are we no longer a queer couple together? Then what are we? I didn't sign up for this, for marriage to a man. Who would want to be a white man in Trump's America? Maybe all the men.

"How does it feel to be straight?" my husband jokes to me. "We're like a hetero couple now." Nothing is funny to me. "You get to be who you want to be," our lesbian friends say to me. "Your husband's gender doesn't determine how you identify yourself. You're still queer, aren't you?" I don't know what I am, what he is.

IN THIS PHOTO: my husband's closet, with stacks of sneaker boxes, so many Cubs baseball caps, aspirational bottles of shaving cream and beard oil.

We live in Boston, a city with a racial wound from the 1970s bus-
ing crisis that is still open and raw, a city where money speaks
but never above a whisper in dark wood private clubs and bars;
a city with tunnels under the Boston Harbor I travel regularly
and every time I am never sure which lane to be in. But Boston
is also a city of 114 colleges and universities, where college students in classrooms introduce themselves by their preferred pronouns and being trans is often not given a second look, a second
thought. Our neighbor's young son makes the switch from big
sister to the cool guy next door with the facial scruff without a
hitch.

One day this past summer, I'm walking behind my husband
to the Forest Hills train station. I'm often walking a step or two
behind my husband. One time in another city, a colleague did
an impersonation of him walking in New York City pretransition, dashing and darting among crowds and obstacles, a blur of
arms and legs, ahead of everyone, a cartoon caricature on fast-
forward. Now I see my husband's father in his quick stride, his
forward posture, even in his careless disregard for my passage
on the sidewalk. *What a fucking asshole,* I think. Nineteen years
together, and now I'm married to a fucking asshole.

I send my husband a flower arrangement at work with a card
that reads *He, His, Him,* but I don't want to be out in public with
him. I don't want to risk another blowup, another evening spent
talking and not talking about variations of masculinity. I don't
want to talk about what he is learning about how to go through a
door, where to stand when he is in an elevator with women, how
to shower at the gym in the men's locker room with a strategi-
cally placed towel around his waist. I go to yoga, I walk the dogs.
I don't write, I don't read, I don't talk to friends.

Our friends in long-standing couples are paying off mortgages, talking about retirement, looking forward to the last kid graduating from college. We make our friends nervous. There is no more easy teasing with my husband about shopping for extra small boy clothes. "Tiny Toy Businessman" I called him when he had a three-piece suit made in Japan, the only place he found clothes to fit his small frame. Friends likely assumed we were past the point of relationship upheaval. Frankly, I thought we were past the point of relationship upheaval too, of separation and division of finances and furniture. They assume my husband is going rogue, that a gender transition at midlife is a kind of breakdown. They don't ask him questions, don't comment on his changing physicality. I feel their refusal to engage as a slap of judgement, against us, against him.

"Can you see my mustache?" My husband is in love with his reflection, with every manifestation of the 150 mg of testosterone he is shooting into his thigh every two weeks. He takes selfie after selfie, records his voice to gauge how it is changing. "You sound like you have a cold," I say cruelly, reveling in being cruel. I start to pant in the drugstore parking lot the first time I pick up his testosterone. I can't catch my breath, I can't get out of the car. I want to drive away, drive off, and go where? Back to when girls were girls and boys were boys? Back to when my husband was my spouse?

My husband and I are having such a terrible time trying to talk to each other that we resort to text messages. We talk through the dogs. Which doesn't seem to help our communication. We text fight and then argue in person, both of us yelling, walking through doorways, in and out of rooms, the dogs head-tilting at us, startled and confused. "Sonny is a man's dog," he says, referring to our Lab rescue. "Because he pees in the bathtub and eats garbage?" I respond. The gendered labeling of everything stuns me into speechlessness. We're all confused. "If you don't want to be with a man, I understand, I do, but I can't be with someone who doesn't love my new body and new masculinity." I JUST MET YOU! I text yell. THIS IS WHO I'VE ALWAYS BEEN! he text yells back.

He tells me the story of the car accident in Orlando again. He was twenty-four. He says he risked the lives of others by driving into traffic to try and destroy himself. "You tried to kill yourself?" This is not a version of the story that I've heard before. "You can't change the story!" I say, bereft. "You can't change the story! This is my story too."

"Maybe you don't tell me some of this," I say. "Maybe you will want to move past us and leave me behind with the weight of all our shared history and memories." What do men at midlife do? They leave, they move on, they start over. With another woman. With a younger woman who has no queer identity, no queer history of unhooking another woman's bra, of making out with women in bars and bedrooms.

I tell people I am past the accumulation and collection stage of life, although I still love to visit antique and secondhand shops. One of my favorite destinations is the Goshen antique mall in Goshen, Indiana, where we stop when we're visiting my husband's parents. There is a stall devoted to typewriters, another with old metal signage, all the old china inherited and then cast off, antique tools and toys. Once we bought a nearly complete set of Fire King peach lustre dishes and a marigold carnival glass pitcher and four tumblers. All winter I set the table in orange to remember the sun, to remember orange was once Carl's favorite color. I don't know what his favorite color is now. Maybe camouflage, maybe steely gray, maybe concrete.

In Goshen my husband bought a trio of painted lead figures we called the Assassins: men in uniform and a woman in a skirt with a briefcase pointing a pistol. She could be me.

What is my story now?

My lover whose name was P— left me. I keep staring at an image of my husband that was taken in a friend's apartment in the summer of 2018: He is slouched in an armless chair, hands in his jeans pockets, his head back, smiling confidently, assuredly. He has a wispy mustache, a hard part shaved into his hair. The photo is a little out of focus as though his image is still emerging. Behind his head is a shadow on the wall. The shadow is small and tentative, hovering over his shoulder. There I am.

the brother

This was what I learned growing up: Boys will build things, shoot
things, climb things, go to war. Girls will pet the cat, maneuver
plastic horses around the living room floor, babysit the youngest brother, gallop across the yellow blanket into the wilderness,
never leave home.

Sons leave home and live in the world, but a daughter is
always a daughter, my mother told me.

These were the cities that grew me up: Buffalo, San Diego, St.
Louis, Williamsville, Florissant.

My brother Mark and I were perched on the gold brocade
couch. Our feet dangled off the edge. I was three and he was two.
We were laughing like a drunk puppy had just walked into the
room. My hair was so curly, so dark—it was animal hair. His hair
was dark and wavy, parted on the right and wet combed. I was
holding Mark's hand. We were beautiful children. We could have

been in an ad campaign for family, the convenience of frozen food, and the American Way.

Christmas, San Diego, 1961. My brother James was four days old. My mother was home from the hospital. There was the silver tree, the blue and white lights. I was five, dressed in a pink multilayer party dress with a wide satin sash, black patent leather shoes. I hated pink. My hair had been temporarily tamed with barrettes and a demure bow. Mark was in a short red jacket and bow tie. He looked like a miniature waiter. There were palm trees outside and no snow. Why weren't we opening our presents in our pajamas? Under the aluminum tree, I was hugging the stuffed black-and-white Dalmatian I got from Santa, but I was looking at Mark's gun and holster and the stiff black felt cowboy hat with the leather lace threaded through a red bead that you could pull tight under your chin.

With two brothers, I was designated sister. I signed their names to the thank-you cards I wrote. It was my duty to be grateful, it was their pleasure to receive. I set the table. I was the child who spoke long distance on the phone to Grandma and the aunts and uncles back in Buffalo, New York. It was assumed that the boys could not be expected to be conversational with relatives, with adults who didn't live with us. Yes, I'm being good. Yes, I help my mother. I lead the Hail Mary when we say the rosary. I set an example. Sometimes it was a bad example.

We were kneeling together on the linoleum in the hallway in front of the Sacred Heart of Jesus portrait for our family monthly devotion. I would rather have been watching *Bonanza* or Walt Disney, anything else than being under the eyes of this Jesus whose gaze followed me, who spied on me wherever my thoughts went. When I stole frozen cupcakes meant for school lunches out of the freezer downstairs, Jesus saw. When I lied and lied—that I had said my prayers and brushed my teeth, that Sheryl Boyer had asked me to her slumber party when she never did—I thought of Jesus's sad eyes. Lying was my go-to. I was afraid of thinking. My thoughts were so messy and unruly. I was afraid that my thoughts—that I—would be judged, that I would be revealed as a bad person, selfish, mean. So I lied. Lying was a reflex, not a calculated choice. I didn't yet believe that being bad was a more interesting way to be. How was it possible to be close to people as myself? I only knew how to be close to people by being what other people wanted me to be. Your brothers are your longest relationships, your biggest supporters, they will always be there for you, my mother told me. *Figghi fai, mariti truovi, frate e sore nun truovi mai.* Children one can have, husbands one can find, but brothers and sisters—one can't find them anywhere, they are a gift of birth. Was she lying? I didn't know if I believed her.

My mother had a younger brother she adored. Their age difference was the same as the difference between me and Mark. Before her brother started balding, he had voluptuous wavy hair and heavy eyes, like an Italian movie star. In a picture, his mouth was soft, but his eyes cut like a switchblade. Everything came to him without asking: money, naïve young girls, women smelling thick with baking yeast and lilac, a full plate at every meal, butter dripping, meat bloody red. He was arrogant and cunning and talked about deals and women like he had easy access to them all. He collected and fixed antique clocks—banjo clocks, mantle clocks, school clocks. He kept time and measured history by tick-ing and bells. It seemed a dedication that should have belonged to a better man, that such a devotion to restoration and precision did not fit a man so careless toward others. I don't remember that he ever asked me a question, or that I saw him pour his wife a cup of coffee. For my mother's whole life, she loved him best, longer than her parents, better than a husband, sometimes so much more than her own sons.

Mark served as an altar boy and rang the sanctus bells during Mass. We chased each other across the altar at St. Thomas the Apostle after Mass. I didn't stop to genuflect or bow my head in front of the tabernacle. I picked up the bells and rang them like I was calling the angels down from heaven.

> *Anyone who claims to be in the light but hates a brother or sister*
> *is still in the darkness.*
> —1 John 2:9

What do you get when you fall in love?

My dad had three brothers. Their parents died within a few years of each other when the boys were still so young they had to raise each other up. Mostly though it was every man for himself: two went off to the service, one took up with a Russian woman who never bent her head toward us to be kissed, the youngest reinvented himself from son and orphan to con man. My dad, the second oldest, tried to do the right thing for everybody, but he couldn't keep his parents alive, couldn't keep the brothers together; he couldn't save the family home. The house was foreclosed for nonpayment of property taxes. Before he shipped out for the Korean War, he wanted someone he could promise to come home to. He wanted to start over and make his own family. He left the shipwreck of his broken family behind.

Mark was a good boy and no trouble. His behavior in school didn't generate calls to our parents from the assistant principal for incomplete assignments or for never coming back to the classroom after lunch. He didn't steal our mother's matches and set fires in the vacant lot or ask a group of sixth-grade girls in the parking lot at school if they wanted to fight. Maybe because there were only eleven months between us and I'd made such an impression with my arrival as the first born, his birth was naturally a letdown. I hoped he'd be called to the priesthood and become a missionary in Africa or Alabama—someplace far away and foreign where we wouldn't have to celebrate our birthdays together anymore.

Growing up, I don't remember who we were to each other. How is that possible when so many people define themselves in relation to their siblings? *My brother, my sister.* My youngest brother James was like the family pet. We opened the door, he went out, we opened the door, he came in. He was an afterthought, a curly-headed boy, eyes like a trapped animal. One day I was sneaking downstairs and left the basement door open, and he fell down the stairs. I caught him before he hit the bottom, but his face was cut, leaving him with a white scar bisecting his eyebrow, another scar on his mouth. Every time I looked at his face, I thought how easy it was to lose hold of each other.

My ultimate sibling fantasy was my friend Donna's family. She had one brother, two sisters. Donna and her siblings went on vacations together. They rented big houses on a beach and cooked together. They shopped together for eyeglasses and special occasion outfits. They babysat each other's kids, sent the drug addict nephew to rehab, sent the drug addict brother to rehab, sent the drug addict nephew to rehab again, moved the gay sister's ex-lover out of the house the other sister owned. Piled the ex's things on the front lawn, changed the locks on the doors. Took notes at each other's doctor appointments, painted each other's kitchens, cleaned each other's basements, loaned each other cars, tools, money. They fought so hard doors slammed, birds fell out of the sky, their familial blood boiled in proximity to each other. They cried in each other's arms, talked to each other every day. How did they find time to go to work? To raise their own families? In my friend Donna's family, husbands, wives, in-laws were all incidental. Their primary relationships were with each other. I looked in on their family and shuddered with longing and sometimes sighed with relief that they were not my family, but when I visited my friend Donna, there was always a photo of me on her refrigerator, on the mantel. Her kids grew up knowing my name.

Anyone who loves their brother and sister lives in the light, and there is nothing in them to make them stumble.
—1 John 2:10

I long to be, close to you

In 1970 we were living in St. Louis. Four students protesting the Vietnam War were killed at Kent State, two antiwar protestors were killed at Mississippi's Jackson State, US bombs were falling on Cambodia, and girls couldn't wear jeans at the high school Mark and I attended. I heard brother and sister Richard and Karen Carpenter opening for Burt Bacharach at the Muny Opera. Karen tapped her drums, so smooth and casual, her brother nodding in approval at her side. As she got skinnier and skinnier, did he feed her, pull treats from his pocket, stop at the drive-through after midnight? Or did he take the food out of her mouth, upend the dinner table, leave her with crumbs?

In 1970 my friends were applying to colleges, talking about senior year plans, graduation, boys boys boys. I skipped rainy days and Mondays the whole month of March my junior year of high school. White flight from the city to the St. Louis County suburbs meant our high school was busting at the seams with students from white families on the run, so the school was split into three shifts to accommodate the student population. Students were coming and going, tripping over each other. I'd leave the house in the morning with Mark and instead of walking to the bus stop, I walked to the end of the subdivision that dead-ended at a farmer's field. I had a book and my lunch that my mom had packed for me, my name on the brown paper bag. I sat on the curb or in the grass at the edge of the field and read all day. I ate the defrosted cupcake. I threw away the orange, the skin knife-scored by my mom for peeling. When school was out, I walked back home.

"How was school today?" my dad asked at dinner.

"A Japanese soldier from World War II was found on an island, twenty-eight years after the war ended. He hid in a cave and waited for the Japanese army to find him." A news story I had heard on the radio while I was setting the table. "He didn't believe the war was over."

"That can't be true," Mark said. "Nobody would be that stupid." We were at such odds that it didn't matter what we believed or didn't, what was true or delusion. We believed what we

believed beyond reason. We both had delusions we would never
surrender.

I believed everything I read in books. Not the monsters, the
magic, the enchantment, not really, but I believed the possibility of everything books promised. I believed it all: that the world
was made up of swirling particles, that fine wine could be dis-
tilled from dandelions, that the canals on Mars once held water,
that a person could float down the Mississippi on a raft to New
Orleans. I was seventeen, skinless. What was I doing? College
students were dying while I read books.

In books, brothers and sisters—the Bobbsey Twins, the
Pevensie siblings from Narnia, the March sisters—lived together
in a pack. They went to war together, solved mysteries, commit-
ted crimes, defeated the bad guys. The oldest brother set the
pace, problem-solved, carried the knapsack. The little brother
was the wayward clown. The sister often sprained an ankle
or had to rip her apron into strips to make bandages. She was
described as a "wet blanket" or a "beauty." The oldest Pevensie
sister lost everything when she chose lipstick over family.

Mark told my parents I wasn't on the bus, wasn't at school. Was
he concerned about my chronic truancy? Did he talk to me before
telling? I don't remember if we ever talked. Did he think that
telling was the right thing to do? The only thing that was right.
Right for me? For him? Would it be possible for us to be close if
we shared delusions, if I thought like him, agreed with him?

My mother bought me a dress that looked just like a dress
Karen Carpenter would wear: high-necked, ruffled collar; cream-

colored lace bodice; long, high-waisted red skirt. I had no idea who I was in that dress. Complete with gloves and a filmy shawl, I wore it like a uniform to a formal dance at a military school. My date was in a uniform of his own, with sashes and gold brocade, a sword at his side. I felt like a prisoner of war next to him.

The summer before drivers' licenses, we did not sleep nights, and Mark and I sneaked out of his bedroom window and met up with Denny from next door and Gayle, radiant as a saint, who was homeschooled by her conservative parents. We longed to be criminals. One hundred and twenty houses were laid out on cul-de-sacs, built around a common ground area that bordered a country club and golf course. We were surrounded by the cover of trees and artificial lawns green as poison. At the end of the street were the new houses under construction. They were in different stages: there were the model homes, the wood-framed houses, the newly excavated basements. We were breaking and entering into the model homes, which was not a violation in our thinking. It was simple to jam a sliding glass door lock with a matchbook cover or a gum wrapper. We walked around the cement block basements, breathed in new paint smells, peeked inside kitchen cupboards, bedroom closets. Once we found a half-empty pint bottle of vodka tucked in a built-in desk drawer next to a bag of Wint-O-Green Lifesavers. Gayle asked me to cut her lush hair, bent her neck. Mark and Denny watched, Denny's attention extended through his freckled arms, his stubby fingers. In an effort to preserve their daughter from the inevitability of sex, Gayle's parents attempted to file a restraining order against Denny. But the scissors were in my hand.

In a photo of my brother Mark from when he was seventeen or eighteen or maybe twenty, he is shaggy and scruffy like a draft dodger or Cat Stevens in his folksy poet days, who Mark listened to in his bedroom on the stereo that he bought with his own money from working at a hospital collecting payment for TV viewing in patient rooms. His was the best stereo in the house. With his door closed, he listened to progressive rock— Emerson, Lake & Palmer; Yes; King Crimson; and big anthem rock like Chicago. I didn't hear what he heard. What was this music about? There was no dirty, sexy lead singer, no lonely, long-haired girl—too many keyboards, not enough sweat. He played guitar in a band in high school although he couldn't play guitar. He often didn't appear in family photos because he was the one taking pictures with his SLR 35mm camera. He owned a motorcycle and a ten-speed bike, ran cross country, wore braces, followed the straight and narrow.

"He's never going to set the world on fire," my mother said about her oldest son. "His ambition in life is to not have to think. I told your father to let him make the decision to pull the plug if I'm lingering on my death bed. He wouldn't think twice to let me go, or your father either for that matter. That's who you want in that situation." Sometimes I admired who Mark was. He owned things, did things. I was envious of his mobility; he could walk streets after dark, run trails; my girlfriends liked him. But not like that. He was not sexy dangerous, he was more thoughtless, circling.

He had had the same girlfriend since ninth grade. She had freckles and long red hair, her ears stuck out when she pulled her hair back. She wanted to study nursing. When Grandma and Aunt Jennie called, they'd ask, "How's Jeanne?" We didn't always understand why she liked Mark, who never gave her birthday cards or took her out on dates, which cost too much money. They hung out. Jeanne helped clear the dinner table, laughed at my dad's weak jokes; my mom said she had a natural beauty. Later, Jeanne picked up with an old, dirty, sexy boyfriend, who was also shaggy and unshaved but in a dangerous way. It was not clear to us if she left Mark or if he was left behind, but she was gone.

Until I could get clear on whether sex was the highway to hell or stairway to heaven, I was hanging out with the Christians— Vicky and Roger, Tom and Bobby. The Christians were always in a pack. They did things like paddle canoes, toast marshmallows over bonfires if somebody remembered the matches, and eat raw cookie dough. Somebody always knew how to set up the tent, somebody always drove; we chipped in for gas. Nobody got drunk and puked on my hair. Nobody grabbed my breasts. There were no flopping dicks flopping around. Tom baked box-mix yellow cake in hollowed out oranges in hot coals, but I felt no heat from any of them even when they prayed out loud and whipped themselves into a saliva-spraying froth. Who were they talking to? I missed dancing. Books were my secret dirty, sexy friends.

If you want her, fight for her, Mark's friends told him, my mother told him. We wanted to fight for Jeanne. She was in all the family photos. I was still setting a place for her at dinner. Mark moved into a crappy apartment with some friends we didn't know. He avoided his old friends. They came over to the house anyway and sat at the dinner table. I sat at the dinner table with a book in my lap. Sometimes I went out with Mark's former friends. In parked cars, basement rec rooms, the family room after parents went to bed, we talked and kissed until we were exhausted, for hours and hours, days. Sometimes we had a kind of sex that may or may not have involved removal of clothing, birth control, or comfort. My dad fell asleep on the couch every night. My mother cooked and cooked, fed everybody.

Nobody went off to college. There was no going away. There was working as a checker at K-Mart, delivering flowers on holidays for a florist. There was working as a car hop at A&W, the indelible smell of onions and fry grease. James grew up scatter-shot and windblown. Mark and I never looked back at him—Did I read to him? Help him with his homework? He was too young and unformed for much speculation, but he held a promise of beauty. He was dark with luminous brown eyes outlined by long, curling eyelashes—*like a girl, like a girl.* My father kept his hair clipped, stifling its natural tendency to grow in cascading ringlets. With short-cropped hair, he was sleek and slippery. He made Grandma nervous because he was so low to the ground and she was afraid she might trip over him. How were we all going to get out of there?

Mark brought a pack of Christians over to my parents' house to eat my mom's spaghetti. They were not my Christians, but like Christians everywhere, they only talked to each other, they looked like they cut each other's hair, they didn't compliment my mother's food, they made inside jokes that only they got. My father poured a glass of wine; Jesus wept. My mother warned Mark about the girl who sat like a frightened tourist on the family room couch, *That girl would make herself a road for you to drive over.* My dad said to Mark, *This family is not broken, why are you leaving? Where are you going?*

This was how I left: I told my parents, my brothers—I'm gay. *Lesbian,* I said.

This was how he left: The girl is pregnant, he said.

At the reception, the girl's parents wouldn't sit until waiters removed bottles of red and white wine my parents had paid for from the tables. I had a lover who was not invited to the wedding. There were no wedding toasts. There was no dancing.

These were my streets: Arkwright Street, St. Paul Avenue, McCarron's Boulevard, 38th Street, 41st Avenue, Fairfield Street, Grampian Way, Columbia Road, Walk Hill Street, Am Sandwerder.

These were my cities: St. Paul, Roseville, Minneapolis, Somerset, Chicago, Boston, Berlin.

These were the things that happened: three children, a farm with fifty chickens, twin pines hissing north, sons without our father's name, long-distance driving, the long distance between us.

That's how girls are, Mark said every time one of his daughters posed or pouted. *Girls like secrets. Girls like pretty things. All girls want to be princesses.* What girls was he talking about? I never wanted to be a princess. I never played with dolls. One of my girlfriends was a repair tech for the phone company. She could strip wires, install phone jacks, climb utility poles. Another girlfriend owned a miter saw, a log splitter. When I visited his house, we talked through his children, "Amy, show Aunt Lynette what you made at church camp."

"David and daddy are going to the car wash. David likes cars and trucks."

Nothing was said that might introduce us to ourselves as adults. I looked around. His second daughter stared at me, her eyes dark and wide. She was eyeing the toy palomino horse with the removable saddle and bridle I had given her. I remembered myself in eighth grade, in jodhpurs and riding boots, my thick, long hair its own untamed entity. "Do you like horses?" I asked her.

"She likes to help in the kitchen, don't you, Em? She's Mommy's best helper."

Everything that was said reflected nothing of my life, or the life Mark and I had shared as brother and sister. My picture never sat on his mantel.

I moved away from the city of men. I built a life around women: I lived with women, loved and fought with women, my friends, my lovers, my family.

These were the years: forty. These were the times my brother Mark crossed my threshold:

In my lesbo community, forty was the cut off age to be single. Since most of us had missed out on a gay adolescence, thanks to homophobia and enforced heteronormativity, we acted out our angsty adolescent romances in our twenties and often well into our thirties. Or we stayed forever with the first woman we slept with, whether as penance for our sins, in profound relief for acting on our desires, or as an enduring reward for the one time we were brave or reckless—after finally landing in bed with a girl, there was no way we were going to risk a new bed, a new girl.

When I was forty, I was single again, paying half the mortgage on joint property where I was no longer living, which meant I couldn't afford to pay rent to live someplace else. It was a matter of basic economics. I was on a ledge, thinking about jumping and making a technicolor smear of my life on the unforgiving ground. I wanted to chop off my hair, tear my clothes, open veins, and paint the walls in Day-Glo heartbreak. So I moved back into my parents' house located in the suburb called Sherwood Creek in far north St. Louis County. I packed my books and computer and left the farm in Wisconsin where I had lived for ten years with the lover who owned the miter saw and the log splitter, and I drove six hundred miles with two screaming cats pulling a four-foot-by-eight-foot U-Haul trailer. I unpacked my office in my old childhood bedroom, the smallest of the bedrooms in my parents' four-bedroom ranch house, the bedroom once painted yellow, the room where my mother closed the heat register and stored the dozen or so varieties of cookies she baked every Christmas. I slept in the double bed my parents had bought for me when I was four, the bed with the maple headboard and footboard, the maple dresser and nightstand.

I had thought that returning to St. Louis would mean that my friend Donna and I would become everyday friends and we'd save the money that we were spending on long-distance calls so we could go out for breakfast and join the Y. I would become integrated into my brothers' lives, starting with unloading the truck. My brothers would help carry the boxes into the house, follow me in a car to the U-Haul place to return the trailer. Then we'd all sit down at my mother's table and eat together. They'd invite me to their kids' soccer games and volleyball games, ask me to babysit. We'd reinvent our sibling relationships without having to travel six hundred miles to see one another.

I originally left St. Louis after high school because St. Louis was big and mean and ugly. This was how I felt when I was in St. Louis: big and mean and ugly. When I returned for a brief period of time at age forty, I was large with grief, huge with homesickness. I hated everything. I was bitter and twisted, four-teen years old, forty years old, living in my parents' house again.

I unloaded the trailer myself. I had packed each box so I could carry it in my own arms, with my own puny strength. Nobody came over for dinner. There was so much food. I ate it all so my mom's feelings would not be hurt. I ate and ate and was still hungry.

I was home every day with my parents, working editing soft-ware manuals, writing a tour guide for Niagara Falls, producing a newsletter for the Minneapolis YWCA, all in my little make-shift office with the particle board desktop. Nobody came over. "When do you have family dinners?" I asked my parents. Birth-days sometimes, the holidays. Why wasn't I cooking family din-ner at my own table?

There is the myth of family, that we will sit at the same table and eat together, that we all know where our scars come from, that we will share our medical histories and memories.

As the Old Italians died—Grandma and all her sisters, Aunt Jen-nie, then the rest of the aunts and uncles one after another, tak-ing with them their recipes and faded housedresses, their garden fountains and antique timepieces—my brothers and I lost our identities as grandchildren, niece and nephews. At long last the impossible happened, and our mother then our father died. We thought they would live forever. We were orphans. The family that remained was a handful of cousins, a husband, exes, wives, our own offspring, our chosen families.

Siblings hold memory for each other, memories of who we were as a first family—me falling backward off the porch at six breaking my wrist, the youngest brother swallowing a screw from a corn popper push toy (I called my father at work while Mom held the baby upside down whacking his back), Mark and I exploring the storm sewer tunnels under our North County subdivision, catching crawdads in the wastewater contaminated creek, Mark and my dad bringing me home the night I was fifteen passed out on gin and Hawaiian Punch at Sioux Passage Park and for the first time realized it was possible to become untethered from time and place, to lose memory.

My brother Mark and I didn't share our memories. "Do you remember . . ." was not in our lexicon.

If he needed bone marrow, a loan, a ride to the airport, rehab, would I put my hand in my pocket, would I drive him where he needed to go, invite him to sit at my table? I have no idea what would soothe him—Our mother's red sauce? Our father's glass of wine? The company of our pet youngest brother? If I can learn to love my husband who used to be my wife, are there possibilities for us—for me and my brother—that we will sit and laugh together again, walk through windows, duck Jesus's sad eyes? Are there possibilities for the red-faced yelling men today? Will you be my brother?

> But anyone who hates a brother or sister is in the darkness and walks around in the darkness. They do not know where they are going.
> —1 John 2:11

Yesterday once more

In a silent family home movie, Mark and I are sitting on the gold brocade couch again. We wear matching red pajamas, and red holiday candles sit on the marble top coffee table alongside a bowl of gold and red ornaments. We let each other go. Mark slides off the couch, stumbles toward the camera. Where is he going? *Good-bye to love.*

the man next door

Our puppies loved each other. When they saw one another—our dog on leash, Stella running through the neighbors' yards—they would rush toward each other moaning, rear up and embrace, mouth wrestling. We loved her too, poor wild garbage dog. She was a little unkempt, a little smelly; she needed brushing, a bath. She was fluffy and shaggy and wild. I'd find her wandering the shared front hallway, inadvertently locked out of her own home, nobody noticing that she was missing.

When a white man starts talking, I wonder how soon before he says something stupid:

Racism goes both ways.

Actually . . .

Nothing will grow here.

I will build a wall.

All boys need to grow up with a dog.

When my husband and I first moved into our two-unit condo in the Jamaica Plain neighborhood of Boston, it was November. We were looking forward to having neighbors. Moving on from

our history of owning single-family homes, and after three years
of apartment living in Boston, we wanted to live with people
in a community that might or might not include a rain barrel,
composting, shared responsibility for raking leaves, raised garden beds, driveway basketball, and barbecues. While unpacking
boxes and organizing the kitchen, I hoped to meet our condo
neighbors, who I'd seen coming and going out the back door:
an attractive, tall, big-bodied woman, her young son, and what I
assumed was the housekeeper. Maybe a mother-in-law in town
for Thanksgiving. A heavy-bottomed figure in a puffy coat and
a knit cap, auburn curls escaping the edges of the hat. "Who is
that?" I asked my spouse, pointing out the middle-aged mother-
in-law getting out of a car.

That's Brendan. The husband.

The florid-faced man who wears the knit cap whatever the
season, whose contribution to what is supposed to be the shared
responsibility of property upkeep is to blow leaves and debris
into heaping piles along the wood fence and to stockpile bags
of winter salt we won't use, who claims after seven years in
their condo that nothing will grow around the perimeter of our
houses—there or there or there—that we are doomed to live on
a bare, salted dirt pad, and who purchases a new lawn sprinkler
every spring for our miniature front lawn that I want to rip up
by its chemically overfertilized roots and replace with a diver-
sified meadow of strawberry clover, chamomile, alyssum, and
English daisies. Where is the sprinkler he bought last season?
How many lawn sprinklers does one household need especially
when there is so little lawn to water? He smokes cigars on the
bluestone patio, outside our open windows, the smoke mingling
with our television watching. When it snows, he cleans off his
car, gets in, and drives off, leaving the woman and child to make
their own way.

Was he once heavy? Heavier than he is now? A fat boy who was teased for his size, his curls, his clumsy features? His young son is beautiful, freckled, with creamy soft skin and vivid green eyes.

"We don't want a rain barrel in the yard," he says, dragging a painted steel fire pit to the middle of the patio. "It will breed mosquitoes." He burns a Christmas tree in the fire pit, and it collects rainwater all spring.

He is a man who, at first glance, is not seen as a man. He is such an unlikely man, or maybe he is the most likely of men. "It's a sausage fest," Brendan says about another golf tournament he is off to, men in whale-print pants swinging sticks, riding in little carts with drink holders across manufactured and manicured green expanses. How is he betrayed by his body? What does he build? What does he make? What does he discover?

He rattles—when we ask him about getting the snowblower we share tuned up for winter, or remind him to close the garage door so fertilizer and insecticides are not accessible to animals and kids, or suggest that it's not a good idea to let a four-month-old puppy run off leash in an urban neighborhood.

It's so easy to hate men these days. White men. White male politicians posturing on horseback, paying out hush money to women they fucked or fucked over, white men spitting on the sidewalk, white men carrying tiki torches marching in white supremacist rallies, white men posturing like experts on subjects they know nothing about, white men reaching down and petting their dicks like the family dog.

When a dog appears in a movie, on a television show, or even in a book, my first thought is, *Does the dog die?*

William Maxwell's tender and nostalgic nonfiction novel, *So Long, See You Tomorrow,* is the account of a murder on a tenant

farm outside of Lincoln, Illinois, in 1923. The second half of the
book is a fictionalized account of the murder from various perspectives, including the viewpoint of the farm dog, Trixie. Trixie
is a fixture who is auctioned off with her farm. The new tenant
will inherit her. Tied to a tree, Trixie mourns the loss of her boy,
her family, howling into the night, night after night.

A dog is a fixture, belonging to a family, a place; a devotion, a
simple pleasure of life, the best part of remembering.

Initially, I was an ambivalent dog owner. I could walk around a
cat, but a barking dog thumping a tail against a hard wood floor,
dropping a wet ball in my lap was a commitment of time and
attention I didn't think I had time and attention for. No talking
babytalk even to babies or lovers, no high-pitched, emotive treat
voice. "Who's a good boy? Who's a good boy? Are you my good-
est, bestest boy?" In my harried grasping for time and space, to
write, to read, to navigate a complex and often confusing world,
dogs were just one more thing. I learned to love dogs because I
fell in love with a person who loved dogs. "Let's cut our losses
before we get in too deep," my husband said on our second date.
"The dogs come with me. We're a package." Every relationship
comes with a package it seems, whether pets or allergies, exes,
child support payments, student loans, or psychic histories of
trauma and neglect.

This relationship started with a team package of a salt-and-
pepper Lhasa mix with a charming underbite that masked his
generally curmudgeonly and occasionally amiable demeanor,
and the jumping licking panting black dog, who on our daily
walks to the river in Minneapolis, the lake shore in Chicago, or
the harbor in Boston, rolled and rolled in the sand, the shore
mud, the salt flats. I learned to live with grit under my feet,

between the sheets. I gave up the standards of home and house-keeping I had previously sought to maintain, the paw-print- and dog-lick-free surfaces, the eradication of animal hair.

There were no private spaces in the little house I moved into with my not-yet husband, no space designated No Dogs Allowed. The black dog followed me everywhere: Are you going to eat? Are you eating? Share? The black dog was an impulse of unregulated energy and enthusiasm. She would chase the stick, chase the stick, chase the stick. She had been surrendered to the animal shelter when she was five months old because she was "too much work." She woke up ready to work every day all day long. She was so young, as young as our untested, untried relationship, and then fifteen years later she was gray-muzzled, dragging her left leg, crashing to the floor in our first apartment in Boston like a bag of sticks, our lives forever changed. I gave in, gave up, and gave over to the uncompromising love of dogs.

The first winter in our new home in Jamaica Plain, our old yellow Lab died (do *all* the dogs die?). That spring we got a puppy, and shortly after, the neighbors got a puppy too. For his son, Brendan said, although the boy was skittish around dogs in general and mostly indifferent to anything he couldn't access from a screen. Every boy should have his own dog, a four-footed, furry best friend, his father said. Having his own dog will teach him responsibility, he will be big brother to a puppy and he and the dog will grow up together, like Brendan did with some dog from his closed history, although we doubted this claim as Brendan seemed so clueless as to the needs and habits of dogs, neighbors, and even his own timid young son. We assumed Brendan grew up with a dog from a television show or a cartoon, like Scooby-Doo or Snoopy, or like a friend who said she had always been

fond of Lady in the Disney cartoon, and not an actual dog that
shed hair everywhere and chewed everything and needed routine and training. The wife, in the manner of overextended wives
trying to set personal boundaries everywhere in every time, told
us the husband wanted the dog, so the dog was the husband's
responsibility.

At Forest Hills Cemetery where I walked everyday with and
without dogs, I regularly visited the graves of Henry and Lucinda
Barnard, who died in 1863 and 1913, respectively. On top of their
flat gravestone is a statue of a larger-than-life Newfoundland. I
don't know if the dog was personal to the Barnards or just a common Victorian grave sculpture. The dog is depicted lying down,
his enormous stone head on his enormous stone paws. In this
final resting place, the dog grave marker seems less about the
couple buried there and more about dogs at rest and not.

The yellow Lab's death was a whisper that we heard deep in our
sleep that startled us awake to the impossibility of life without
a dog. Life with at least one dog was now our normal, a daily
tether to both routine and abandon—walks and feeding, play and
surprise: A squirrel! A treat! A friend! We had moved four times
since our first dogs together. We had culled boxes of books, closets of clothes, and files of old correspondence, but the urns and
boxes of pet cremains moved with us. The first questions we had
looking at a new place were "Is there a yard?" and "Where can
we walk the dogs?"

After the yellow Lab died, I took the new curly-headed puppy to
meet the stone dog at the cemetery and left a treat between his
massive paws. The puppy barked and bowed as though she could

wake the perpetually sleeping dog from the grave, as though she could will a resurrection of all the dead dogs.

The neighbors' puppy's name was Stella, which seemed apt as she was yelled at so often, so emphatically. We called her the Garbage Dog. She was a blonde teddy bear, eager to please, happy—but these people with a dozen years of graduate and professional education between them had no business with a puppy. They brought the puppy home on a Sunday and left to go to work Monday morning—an easy ten-hour day for both of them. They didn't understand why she peed and pooped all over the house, why they had no success house or crate training her, why she didn't eat the food that they left out all day next to the always accessible water bowl, why she chewed shoes and eyeglass cases and TV remotes, why she dragged the young son all over the yard wherever she wanted to go until he tripped and fell flat on his face and then refused to walk her on leash anymore.

They opened the back door and let her out into our unfenced asphalt yard behind a busy through street. The first time I was digging in the front yard in an effort to restore the hypothetical sterile dirt and the Garbage Dog ran toward me full tilt, cars zooming by at my back, I screamed her name like Marlon Brando in *A Streetcar Named Desire*—"Stella!"—then tackled her before she got to the curb. Shaking, sweating, I led her by the collar around to the back. Brendan was sitting on the patio, earbuds in, reading a golf magazine. "She was heading for the street," I said, trying to be informative without yelling. Brendan looked up, tucking a curl under his knit cap, and started to rattle: "She knows better than to go in the street . . ." He rattled on and on.

Is there anything more impenetrable than a stupid man's certainty about a subject he knows nothing about? Is there anything less present tense than a misplaced nostalgia for a fictionalized time and place when boys and dogs ran together in backyard woods?

We sent the wife information for dog walkers, dog trainers, dog groomers; I suggested that we attend a group puppy training class together. But I learned part of getting along with the neighbors, especially neighbors my husband and I shared walls and a yard with, was respecting boundaries. While we all could share garden overflow and outrage at the national news, and while Carl and I could appreciate the foil-wrapped slices of cherry pie and coconut cake the wife, who was a gifted baker, left for us on the hallway table, the puppy's welfare was an issue of marital roles and responsibilities between them and not one we could address more directly.

Brendan's favorite thing to do with Stella was to load her into his Volvo, open the back windows all the way, the dog unsecured by a leash or harness, and drive to J. P. Licks or the Boston Public Garden or the Boston waterfront—someplace that was crowded with people who all took one look at the blonde bouncing puppy and wanted to pet and cuddle her, coo baby talk at her, at Brendan, who preened and beamed as though Stella's cuteness was a direct reflection of his own far-fetched irresistibility.

I conferred with a dog-walking friend about the risks of dognapping. I had a key to the neighbors' house, the puppy could just . . . disappear one day while Brendan and Karen were at work, their son at school. Would any one have noticed?

A four-month-old puppy that doesn't know the difference between a stone dog and the real deal might know her name if she's lucky, might know that everything is delicious, but can't be expected to distinguish between the car that takes you to the park where you run with your friends and the car that runs you over.

Like Skip and Old Yeller, Old Dan and Little Ann, like Trixie, sweet Stella was a goner.

Before I could act on the dog abduction plan, after more close calls than we could count, after repeated warnings and threats, after Stella was found wandering blocks away from home again and again, she was killed by a hapless driver as she ran across the street. It was a summer weekend. The whole neighborhood was out. If we didn't see it, we all heard it. Brendan was the only one who was surprised. While one of the competent and decisive lesbian couples on the block pulled their car up and loaded Stella inside, while my husband drove the too-calm but quivering wife to the emergency animal medical center—*I told him I told him I told him*—and I took the young son inside to distract him with cartoons, Brendan collapsed onto his hands and knees on the dog-pee-bleached grass sobbing and sobbing. It's so easy to hate men these days. "Get yourself together, man," a neighbor on a bike said, reaching down and petting Brendan's heaving shoulder.

Is it possible for what is done to be undone? Can a nostalgia for what might have been create new narratives from other perspectives for the sake of healing, for the sake of "get[ting] back to the place [we] hadn't meant to leave," or will it leave us trapped in lingering and paralyzing grief? When do we scatter the ashes of the dead dogs?

It is early garden season again here in Jamaica Plain. After the long winter, I am planting beets and arugula, Fortex pole beans and collards at my community garden plot. In the flower beds with amended soil around the house, the Munstead lavender plants are coming back, red and pink azaleas are in bloom, and there is a Wine & Roses weigela that I will move to a spot with more sun. I am walking in the cemetery with our two dogs, the black one and a new yellow one, the dogs young, me not young but all of us so happy for new grass and sun, for leash walks and balls, dog friends, the Canada geese at the cemetery pond and delicious goose poop. Last week, the neighbors texted and sent us a video of a puppy, white as a shroud, playing in grass. Guess who arrives next weekend? the text said.

We compose a simple note: "We are leaving town this weekend with the dogs. To tell you the truth, we have very mixed emotions about the arrival of a new dog and we'd rather not be around. The situation with Stella traumatized us. We want to continue to be good neighbors, but we can't be excited about or involved with another dog. We are completely stressed out and worried. We don't want to be judgmental or unkind in any way but rather need to protect ourselves. We hope for the best."

A dog drags us into the world, insisting I am yours and you are mine, now, let's go for a walk.

The curly-headed black dog and I are attending a group dog training practice at the Harvard Arboretum, which is near our house. Yellow forsythia are nearly spent and rhododendrons, a cliché New England flowering shrub that is as short-lived as a New England spring, are gearing up to bloom. The puppy jumps straight up in the air when she encounters a blue jay feather, a dandelion seedhead, a sneaky stick; on trash day she must duck and crawl around the trash bins on the sidewalk. There is danger everywhere. Where is her messy friend? I stumble on the path, weave and wander, stare at my feet. My unsteady pace trips her. She walks around my legs. Training protocol is that dogs are not to greet each other, so all the dogs and their owners stand in a large half circle a little distance from each other in a short grass meadow attentive to the young blonde woman who assesses our posture, our breathing: Stand up straight! Lower your hands! Head up! Shoulders back! Breathe! Sit your dogs! We pant at her feet. We are all tethered to one another.

What is our responsibility for the death of a dog? For the death of any living thing? If I am walking at Forest Hills Cemetery and the Garbage Dog comes running toward me, will we pass each other and keep going as though we'd never met? If I see her in a stone grave marker with her goofy laughing face, will I reach in my pocket, toss a treat offering, and then turn away?

When the new white puppy comes bounding toward me, toward my dogs, all tangled in their leashes, everyone barking *Hello! Hello!,* and I see Brendan in his ambiguous body with his unflagging certainty, rattling in his deep denial sickness, will I turn away in my hate for him, or will I pick her up, and will we run and run?

becoming queered

Like any origin story, there is never one story. There is the story I tell myself, the story I told my mother, the story I tell my lovers, the story my dreams tell me, the story I am telling you now from this distance about what "queer" meant to me, about how I became queer, and the women who made me.

Birds fly over the rainbow
Why then, oh, why can't I?

i. judy: longing for home

When I was eleven, living in St. Louis, I discovered you could check out LP record albums from the public library. My brother Mark and I had our own bedroom stereos, a turntable, and two speakers. We weren't big on sharing, and our tastes in music reinforced our individual listening. My first LP was by Herman's Hermits, which sparked debates with my girlfriends about the merits of the Hermits versus the Monkees versus the Beatles. It didn't seem a fair fight to me. The Beatles were in a singular category. I knew that at eleven. I wanted to listen to the Rolling Stones, but I felt no entry point to their music. Not as a young girl listening to "Under My Thumb" or the Stones' lesser hit, "Stupid Girl." I was curious about Bob Dylan, but I couldn't afford to buy record albums often. With what few dollars I made babysitting, collecting my allowance, what if I bought a whole album and only liked one or two songs? A waste. So I checked out records from the library, where my options were limited to mostly classical recordings, a frontier unknown to me except for a few things I'd heard in a sixth-grade music appreciation class like *Peter and the Wolf* and *The Nutcracker*. The local library had a hit-or-miss music collection of contemporary pop music— Barbara Streisand, Johnny Mathis, Frank Sinatra, Judy Garland—who I knew of course from *The Wizard of Oz,* which was how I wound up checking out the 1964 live double album of Judy Garland and Liza Minnelli at the London Palladium.

I played the album on repeat. I listened to meet my own moodiness, not to be uplifted or perked up. Sometimes I skipped the overture of hits: I skipped "The Trolley Song." Most of the time, I skipped "Zing! Went the Strings of My Heart." I skipped "San Francisco" and "Chicago." I gravitated to big emotion, but not belting: I listened for the catch in the throat, the tremolo and gasp—"The Man That Got Away," "The Music That Makes Me Dance," "Once in a Lifetime," "Never Will I Marry." I didn't understand the origin of emotion. At the time, I thought all emotion came from a longing for home.

Growing up in six houses in as many cities in three states, I heard a refrain, a constant trickle of sound, through all the years of my childhood: *I want to go home.* My mother recited this litany from the time I was five years old and we left our first home in Buffalo, New York, in 1960 and moved to the West Coast. No matter where we were living, Buffalo was always home—where blood, hot peppers, red wine, and hard-crusted bread were familiar, where everybody lived on a bus line.

"Grandma told me my place was with my husband, so I left Buffalo. Now every day I have regret. To live with regret is a terrible thing. It bends your head, clouds your eyes. Music is all the same song it hurts to hear."

My mother never wavered in her conviction. Wherever she was living, her home was Buffalo.

I didn't understand my mother's grieving for Buffalo—for a people, a place, a landscape of bars and bowling alleys, clam stands along Niagara Street—but I felt her loss as a palpable sadness that infected my life, that judged anywhere other than Buffalo as inadequate.

My mother was a few years younger than Judy Garland, and I thought my mother resembled her. They were both small women, barely five feet tall with short auburn hair, and at different times, my mother and Judy looked too skinny, they smoked too much, drank too much. Judy's drug abuse had been encouraged by the MGM studio system, the amphetamines and barbiturates, pills to wake her up or put her to sleep. My mother supplemented vodka martinis and brandy Manhattans with lithium, valium, a bottomless coffee pot that kept her vibrating with anxiety—"nerves" it was called, drifting toward the breakdown lane. My mother had also been a singer—so she told us—until the cigarettes corrupted her voice. While working as a salesclerk in Buffalo before her marriage to my father, she had been a member of the J. N. Adam department store women's choir. She loved to sing, loved music, although she was not a fan of Judy's. While my mother lived in an emotional landscape of dramatic highs and lows, she thought there was something a little undignified about Judy's full-throated emoting, the wet eyes, quivering mouth; too vulnerable was not attractive or feminine according to my mother. In my mother's case, that vulnerability was camouflaged by an anger that kept people at a distance. She liked Dionne Warwick singing Burt Bacharach, the smooth coolness of Chuck Mangione's flugelhorn—a cloudless sky, without ripples or turbulence.

There was also Judy's status as a gay icon, a beacon leading me to my destiny, not that I had any idea at eleven that the term "friend of Dorothy" was a code gay men used to identity each other. Not that I had any idea what "gay" meant. Gay men were Garland's biggest fans, including two of her five husbands.

I wanted to be Judy Garland's daughter. I wanted to save her from danger with my body. I thought there could be no finer existence than to sit at Judy Garland's feet, looking up at her in adoration, to bask in the reflected glow of her shine and sparkle. Like Liza, who looked like a baby giraffe next to Judy, I was bigger than my mother. Where she was petite, slim as a cigarette holder, I was a puff ball with scraped knees and a constellation of wild dark hair that lifted me beyond my own Italian girlhood, above virgin martyrs and Madonnas. When I listened to Judy and Liza, I could hear their complicated love, their jealousy and rivalries, the threat of suicide by mother, the expectation of salvation from daughter. Women were bound to each other by broken dreams, by whiskey and cigarette-scarred voices, by the bad treatment of men.

And suddenly you're older

When I listened to Judy, I was hearing every woman's song. I was hearing my mother's song and the voices of the J. N. Adam department store women's choir.

My mother was not a happy woman. Her sadness was like listening to a foreign language opera. I could feel the grief, her sorrow, but I could not understand the story, the relationships between characters, the narrative arc. Her sadness seemed much bigger, more unwieldy than any meaning I could assign to it. When she was not sad, she was most often angry. Like her sadness, her anger seemed without clear cause or relief. Judy gave voice to a longing that made sense to me, that reflected her own dramatic rise to becoming one of the greatest entertainers of her time.

ii. elizabeth taylor: the queer body

Men have been staring at me and rubbing up against me since I was twelve years old.

—Liz Taylor as Laura Reynolds in *The Sandpiper*

For young girls, sex was mixed up and confused with a definition of beauty. As young girls, we are our bodies. We learn our first lessons about power and powerlessness, about how the world will receive us, from our own faces and bodies.

In the intimate world of my family, beauty was often identified as a quality seemingly synonymous with goodness and exquisite style. Souls were beautiful; Father Donatelli was a "beautiful servant of God." Table settings could also qualify as beautiful as well as music. Beauty as it applied to women was most frequently divided into parts, distinct and separate from the person: beautiful hair, skin, teeth, eyes. When Jo sold her hair in *Little Women* to make a financial contribution toward the comfort of her sick father, Marmee lamented the reckless sacrifice of Jo's "one beauty." Physical beauty was evidence of God's special favor, a blessedness of spirit that resisted the necessity to be anything more and could not be bought at any price. The message I received growing up was that for women, it was always preferable to be pretty rather than smart. Which somehow I understood to be about survival, about being allowed to survive, allowed by men, who held power over women's lives, like the power to say where we lived, even though the men around me couldn't seem to do the simplest things—remember to pick up milk or iron a shirt or make their own dentist appointment. They made money, sometimes, and just as often, lost it on bad deals and bad bets, or spent it on loud cars and golf clubs. And the women—the housewives referenced in Betty Friedan's *The Feminine Mystique,* which I had read an excerpt of in junior high; the women in *Valley of the Dolls,* a book I found at a neighbor's house while babysitting; and my own great-aunt Florence, who left her husband or who was left—were depressed and unfulfilled and drank too much and took too many pills. My mother was depressed. She said her depression was about homesickness for Buffalo, but maybe her depression was the result of her disempowerment by the patriarchy, maybe she was another depressed housewife among the generations of depressed housewives. Perhaps the condition of *housewife* was the forerunner of depression, a condition it made sense to me to avoid.

BEAUTY AS FEMME-BOY

In *National Velvet,* young Elizabeth Taylor in riding breeches and a hard hat passed as a beautiful young boy, a femme-boy.

Liz Taylor the femme-boy wraps her legs around the manic, jumping cart horse she wins in a raffle. She rides in the Grand National. In the movies in my head, sometimes I am Liz Taylor lying unconscious, pale, and disheveled on the muddy track, dressed in jockey drag, a beautiful boy about to be revealed as a beautiful girl. Sometimes I am the attendant nurse in starched white and soundless shoes, loosening Liz's collar, unbuttoning her jockey silks, dreaming cool starched white dreams, my cool soft hands trembling with erotic discovery. Sometimes I am Mickey Rooney as Mi Taylor, the fallen jockey, Liz's trainer, making my way from stable to stable, a girl disguised as a sly, slick, opportunistic orphan. I am cutting Liz's hair. Scissors flash and Liz's glossy black curls litter the straw like dead animals. My hands are on the exposed pale stem of her neck. When Liz falls, she lands in my arms.

ITALIAN GIRL COUSINS, SUMMER 1968

Italian girls mature early. I'd been hearing that since the appearance of my breasts and first bra. I had no idea what their appearance meant for my future. I just knew that when I was eleven, they disrupted my present. When I thought of growing up, I thought of smoking, spitting, practicing billiards, driving a car. I thought of the heroics of sex, of desperate, undying love, of a cavalry of beautiful lovers on beautiful horses galloping toward me. I did not think of china and crystal patterns, of church weddings and orange blossoms. I thought of the commercial on television: A woman with hair blowing in the wind running in slow motion in a waving grass meadow or along a beach at sunset toward a man with brown hair and a beefy face who stands and waits. *I can't seem to forget her. Her Windsong stays on my mind.* From the edge of the scene, she would never see me coming toward her.

I was an Italian girl, like Carmella and Yvonne, younger sisters of my cousin Connie's husband Dominic. They were the most mature girls I knew, but then they lived in Buffalo, New York, in the city, where the street came right up to your front door and there were no garages to shelter your bike. My breasts and bra were no big deal to Carmella and Yvonne. In fact, they were more likely to think I was a little backwards, a Missouri hillbilly, a Bald Knobber character from the Ozarks, which is how I felt in their presence. I was the bushy-haired, tight-boned stranger from the Midwest boonies. Carmella and Yvonne were the Golden Girls. Their honey-colored skin never looked oily, their gold-streaked hair, never frizzy. Their forearms and upper lips were smooth and hairless. They were sleek and glowing; there was a rosy pulse under their skin that made me want to warm my hands on them.

Every summer we visited our Buffalo family. The point of our long-distance pilgrimages was to enforce our sense of extended family affiliation—to know and be known. I grew up believing that ethnicity was dependent upon place, not only where you or your grandparents were born but where you lived. I can't remember a time when I didn't know what I was: I was Italian. My grandparents were born in Italy and Sicily. My parents were born in Buffalo, New York. I was born in Buffalo. In Buffalo we were Italian, among our people, in our place. The rest of the country was a vast white, flat-faced Protestant wasteland.

The summer I was eleven, I was sitting at dusk on the front steps of the row house where Carmella and Yvonne lived, the backs of my thighs sweating, watching Carmella paint her toenails in the yellow light that spilled from the hallway.

The world had turned since I had seen them a year ago, and Carmella had gone boy crazy, from a backyard puddle to Niagara Falls, coming home branded with love bites after midnight, shaving her legs past her knees, shaking boys out of her pockets like loose change—young boys on bicycles, older boys in big cars, a soldier with a creepy crewcut.

Carmella's golden head was bent over her toes. "I'm too young, for one boy, to go steady," she said as she applied the polish in sure deliberate strokes, "but there is one. I like him so far the best."

I understood the longing to ride away into the sunset, toward love and distance, my hair wild in the wind, my legs shaved past my knees, but what was it to have a boyfriend? To like boys? To like one boy the best?

"One day you're a kid and everybody looks past you, over your head," Carmella went on. "And then one day it all changes and men look at you, and only you, like they've never seen you before."

That's the way I looked at Carmella. Her name reminded me of caramel: soft, chewy candy. Carmella had no discernible bones. Day after day, as I struggled against gravity, feeling my body too big for my bones, my bones crashing inside my shell of skin, Carmella was a thick syrup, fluid and seamless. I didn't understand the changes that Carmella referred to, but I felt some essential heat from her, a pulling that attracted and disturbed.

Carmella had crossed some great divide, leaving me and Yvonne scuffing our tennis shoes in the playground dirt on the other side. *Take me with you!* I wanted to call out to Carmella. Her sexual power was like the 750,000 hydroelectric gallons of water pouring over Niagara Falls every second, lighting up all of New York state and Ontario.

Carmella capped the polish, stood, and stretched. "You don't know," she said earnestly. "You don't know. I want to wait, but sometimes I wonder. What would it matter? If not this one, then someone else, you know?"

We all admired Carmella's toes, painted red as the new blood in our Italian girl panties.

"In *To Kill a Mockingbird,* a Black man is accused of raping a white woman . . ." I was telling my mother about the book on my lap. "There's no such thing as rape," my mother said. She licked her thumb and tried to smooth my unruly eyebrows, which made me jerk my head away from her. "A woman always has a choice. She can choose to die." "Never go anywhere alone," my mother told me over and over. "Never leave this house unless I know where you're going and when you'll be back." In my mother's view, the world was hostile or at best indifferent. Every encounter was about danger, life and death. I was in peril. My life was at risk. I could choose to die. I didn't say it, but I thought, *I could also choose to live.*

BEAUTY AS BEACH BAIT

In *Suddenly Last Summer,* Elizabeth Taylor in a one-piece white bathing suit runs out of the ocean toward a white sand beach. The water is an open expanse, a bare stage, an empty dance floor. Liz sinks to her knees on the beach framed by the white hot sun, the white hot sand, the white bathing suit. Behind a chain-link fence separating the private from the public beach, a crowd of young men and boys presses forward. In their faces, in the forward thrust of their bare-chested bodies, there is a hunger, fierce and fixed. They look at Liz with a ferocity of attention, with cannibalistic eyes, with ravenous hands and mouths.

THE PRINCESS

In the book piles by my bed, on my dresser, balanced on my lap at the dinner table, one of my favorite characters when I was growing up was Dan, the orphan renegade from Louisa May Alcott's *Little Men*. Dan was the dark outsider, who swore, smoked, and split wood in a futile effort to control his temper. Among the tepid-blooded boys at Plumfield, Dan was an open flame, to my mind, the quintessential hero: no family obligations, no societal constraints; loud, fierce, strong-willed, and generous spirited. What a disappointment it was that Dan chose to direct his passion toward the golden-haired, frail jewel daughter of Laurie and Amy, the quintessential princess: prim, proper, a shot of Novocain to the nervous system. Dan, the bad boy, splitting logs and heads, didn't stand a chance for the princess, and neither did I.

Cousin Diane was my princess, and she was beautiful.

Five years older than me, Cousin Diane was tall and painfully thin, with cascading auburn hair, a dark mole on her upper lip, and imperfect teeth that gave her a sweet, shy smile. At seventeen, she had a league of suitors and a family-approved, twenty-five-year-old boyfriend who promised Uncle Leonard, her father, that he would wait until Diane was eighteen before buying her a ring.

It was considered for the best for Diane to marry young, as something about the fact of her being beautiful put her at risk. Although Uncle Leonard paid the costly tuition to keep her in the private all-girls Catholic school and Diane's three brothers hovered over her like bodyguards, she was somehow both in danger and dangerous. There was something about being beautiful that seemed to grant others access to her. Her beauty compelled them to comment, to notice. At family gatherings, while Diane sat silent, coiled over a coffee cup, her appearance was routinely discussed and dissected. "She came downstairs in a skirt so short, I told her, where do you think you're going? You're not leaving the house dressed like that. Every day, boys follow her home. They stand in the street sniffing like dogs—a beautiful daughter breaks a father's heart."

I adored Diane with the kind of intensity only the very young have energy or innocence for. I wanted to brush her long red hair that crackled and sparked like a live flame. She never noticed me. I was her kid cousin. It didn't matter. I loved her because of how she *looked*. It seemed enough.

The summer I was twelve, on another visit to Buffalo, I was in Diane's bedroom at Uncle Leonard and Aunt Angela's house sitting on the edge of her twin bed watching Diane get ready for a date. She was going out with Tom, the man she would announce her engagement to at Christmas, the man she would marry, who would become her first husband.

"It takes three days for my hair to really dry," Diane confided to me as she performed some intricate maneuver to her bangs with a round brush and a can of hair spray. Being beautiful seemed to require an inordinate amount of effort and energy. "And I have a headache every day from sleeping on rollers. At night I rub lotion on my hands and wear cotton gloves to bed— after sixteen your skin starts to lose its natural moisture."

I admired her dedication, her devotion to the physical self, which I interpreted as love of the physical. As a kid I believed that our obsessions defined us: that people who ate a lot loved to eat, that people who looked and looked at themselves in mirrors loved what they saw.

I studied the picture of Tom on the mirror above Diane's dresser. He had shaggy brown hair and a big, beefy face. In the picture, he was leaning against the door of a small red car, probably a sports car. I didn't know if he was cute or not. I had met him a few times without noticing him. One thing was certain, he was a man, not a kid. He drove—his own car. He wanted to marry Diane. In deference to Uncle Leonard's dictate, he was waiting for her.

"What will you do after you get married?" I didn't understand a life plan aimed toward wedlock. The future I could conceive of might involve getting my driver's license, learning how to water ski, wearing contact lenses, visiting France. I didn't see a future with a husband.

"Have sex finally, I guess," she said, giggling nervously, and squirted her neck and wrists from one of the bottles on her dresser. "Here, want a hit?" She handed me the bottle and then rubbed her wrists together briskly. In front of the mirror, she reached under the high-necked short cream knit dress she was wearing to run her hands up her long legs and refasten the off-white fishnet stockings to her garter belt. Her dress was sleeveless, and her bare arms were too naked, fleshless. She slipped her arms into a short cream-colored crocheted jacket and arranged her heavy hair over her shoulders. Around her neck hung a gold chain strung with a golden crucifix. "I don't mind waiting—to have sex, I mean," she sighed, patting her flat stomach. "To tell you the truth, it scares me sometimes to think about it." I could

feel her fear like an animal presence lurking in her bedroom,
lying in wait in her body, although I didn't understand. There
was no fear in Carmella, just a heavy anticipation, a barely contained impatience. Don't go, I wanted to tell Diane. Stay here. I'll
keep you safe. I'll save you.

A family vacation at Table Rock Lake. A rare photo of me in a
bathing suit without a cover-up, sitting on the edge of a pool at
a hotel. When I was eleven, twelve, at the suburban public pool
or a backyard pool party, I wouldn't take off the short terry cloth
robe or the long T-shirt I wore over my bathing suit to hide my
alien body. In the photo, my shoulders are hunched over my
chest, and even from this distance I can feel that I am holding in
my belly; I'm tan and glistening, there are water droplets poised
on my dark eyelashes. I could be on the edge of crying or diving
in, floating or drowning.

I thought the built-in shelf bra in my bathing suit accentuated
my breasts to a prominence that was horrifying, so I wouldn't
take off the cover-up. I resisted wearing the 34B bras my mother
stocked in my top drawer. I was so embarrassed by my body's
runaway early maturity that I couldn't bear any kind of attention to or notice of my physical presence. I wouldn't volunteer
answers in class, and I hated oral presentations or anything that
had a performative aspect to it—drama, debate, sports. One time
in sixth-grade gym class, I was supposed to execute a simple cho-
reographed exercise routine to the song from the movie *Exodus,*
so the night before, I hit my hand with a hammer on the basement floor. My plan was to break a finger and get excused from
gym class, but the pain shocked me into compliance, and I went
to class with a bruised hand. I wore my lush dark hair pulled

back in a low, tight ponytail every day of sixth and seventh grade. I was sure that if people were looking at me, they were looking at my breasts or my wild hair, that I was being assessed as prey or product. It didn't matter if that judgment was intended as admiration or desire. I didn't want it. I was terrified of the attention of boys, men, which I'd been the reluctant recipient of since I was eleven. I wanted to be braver, able to cauterize my own bullet wound, pull an arrow from my side, open a vein, but I was a young girl who wanted to like and be liked by other people, who couldn't smash my hand to save myself, and who was confused when other people's liking me manifested as sexual desire, revealing a sexuality I didn't even know I possessed.

BEAUTY ON BOTH SIDES OF A SEXUAL DIVIDE

As the ultra-femme drag queen Maggie the Cat in *Cat on a Hot Tin Roof,* Elizabeth Taylor in a slippery, shining, tight white slip stalks her beautiful homosexual husband, played by Paul Newman. "You got a nice clean smell about you," she purrs, rubbing against Paul Newman's resistant back. Paul gulps bourbon, hops one-legged, dragging a crutch and a crush on a suicided linebacker. Liz Taylor as Maggie the Cat pouts and purrs, flirts and flounces, steams and sighs, wasting away. She could carry the ball for a whole football team. "There is life in this body," Liz Taylor lies, and we believe her.

There was a weight to beauty, a burden. In the movies in my head, I was lithe, coltish, a girl passing as a young boy. In one movie, I wanted to see the terror and blood on the woman on the beach so I could feel what she felt too, or convince myself that we were close, connected to each another. In another, I lied and

lied, saying what everybody wanted to hear to make everybody
want me.

Beginning in December 2010, over the course of six months,
the self-proclaimed dyke documentary photographer Catherine
Opie photographed Elizabeth Taylor's Bel Air home and possessions "to make a portrait of Liz Taylor through her things." Opie
took three thousand photos of the items on Liz's nightstand, her
artwork, closets, jewelry, shoes, handbags, stuffed animals. The
photos are an image of an image. The project became part intimate study of the details of a star and part memorial, as Taylor
died while Opie was still taking pictures. There is something so
queer in this setup: Liz Taylor, an icon of femininity and a favorite with gay men for her glamour and her advocacy to improve
the lives of people dying of AIDS and raise money for a cure,
and Catherine Opie, in whose self-portrait an image of two stick
figures in skirts and a house with a curl of smoke coming out of
the chimney has been freshly carved into the skin of her back. A
portrait of simple lesbian domesticity in blood. A version of what
it takes to make a queer life.

iii. linda ronstadt: when will i be loved?

Several months after my spouse and I got married in 2012 in
Boston following the legalization of gay marriage in Massachusetts, we hosted a big fat wedding party in Minneapolis, where
we had lived for two decades. My spouse, who had not yet transitioned from my wife to my husband, was ready with a bespoke
suit and shirt, a tie shortened so it wouldn't hang past his belt.
I had an image of what I wanted to look like: retro, floral-print
tea-length dress, red and black, a flower in my hair—a camellia.
It wasn't until I was looking at pictures from the party that I

realized that I had basically recreated one of Linda Ronstadt's iconic images from the seventies: the flowy print dress with cap sleeves, the flower in her hair.

Performance artist John Kelly's obsession with opera diva Maria Callas led him to create a character who was the fictional daughter of Callas and Aristotle Onassis, who he called Dagmar Onassis. In 1984 he made a film adaptation of his live performance where he played Dagmar, in punk drag, and lip-synched as Callas—the desperate self-destructive daughter, the incandescent mother. His performance is drag as embodiment, as divine possession. At my gay wedding I created a character who impersonates Linda Ronstadt, my own version of a love that could save me.

I am not in the market
For a boy . . .

I started listening to Linda Ronstadt with her 1977 album *Simple Dreams*. I had heard her Top 40 hits, "When Will I Be Loved" and "It's So Easy," all over the radio, but they were not songs that interested me. Maybe because I had heard them so many times, maybe because I didn't believe what Linda was singing. At the time, I was writing music criticism for a regional entertainment paper. I was listening to records that arrived by the carton; I went to concerts three nights a week. I was cutting and sharp on the page, but if I wasn't engaged with the music, I had a hard time writing about it, and the only music I cared about in those days was music by long-haired folkie girl singers, or wan white girl singers, or raging druggie girl singers.

I was too uninformed, too immature to understand the art

of interpretation or arrangement. Singers like Judy Garland and Dionne Warwick were different. The songs they sang became their own. Some of the songs Linda sang I'd heard other singers sing, which made me think hers was a lesser art form. But as I listened—obsessively, with headphones on, headphones off, on vinyl and cassette, sitting on the living room floor listening to the RCA console stereo, driving for hours in the 1970 Plymouth Valiant with the Pioneer under-dash radio cassette player and Jensen speakers in the back that my brother James had installed in anticipation of getting his driver's license—she sang me a whole life—looking for love, falling in love, heartbreak, in which I was able to see my own.

I listened like it was my job, my dream job, the soundtrack to the job I trained my whole life for; show up early, stay late; work to make a living, to make a life.

I didn't know music as much as I knew obsession, how to submerge myself in an image, a line, bury myself in the phrasing and harmonies, take on an emotion as my own. I learned everything I knew about the compulsivity of attraction, the incessant whine of possibility, and heartbreak from Linda Ronstadt. I spent years staring at her 1976 *Hasten Down the Wind* album cover, her bangle bracelets and bare, tan shoulders, her breasts under the sheer muslin dress. I was the shadow on horseback behind her. I was out to sea on the background ocean. I was never in the picture, which didn't stop me from dreaming myself into the scene. When I should have been going to econ lectures and French lab my first go-around at college, I sat in one of the student study lounges, not even a book open on my lap, dreaming myself into the picture.

At eighteen, nineteen, the future was unimaginable to me. I had never gone to the same school for more than a year. My family had moved from Buffalo, New York, to San Diego to St. Louis to Buffalo and back to St. Louis, where I started high school. Were we staying in St. Louis this time? Long enough for me to make friends? If we moved again, if I moved, I'd need a new identity, a new escape route, another way out.

"This is the world we live in," my father said. He was driving me to Kmart, where I worked as a cashier. "You got to have medical insurance. If anything happens, you get sick or you're in an accident, you get hurt . . ." What was he talking about? I couldn't imagine a scenario where any of those things might happen, but my dad sounded too serious to argue. "Are you ready to get a full-time job?" At Kmart? What was he talking about? "You can stay on our insurance if you go to college." I was at risk of not graduating from high school due to skipping the month of March my junior year. My dear, sweet, desperate father talked to me about The Future and health insurance and ruining my life.

I had to get myself into a college, any college, any way I could, which was the only way I could stay on my parents' health insurance. Or, I could join the Navy. He had picked up brochures from a Navy recruiting office. I saw the brochures on the kitchen table. In 1946, when he was just seventeen—the age I was when he talked to me—my father anticipated being drafted into combat as soon as he turned eighteen, and so he received permission from his father to join the Navy. He served as a radio operator on board a transport ship. How did the immigrant working-class young men stay alive during a war? Their loyalty was to their families—the families they were born into, who thought of their American children as money in the bank, and to their future families, the ones they were dreaming into being. In my parents' worldview, military service would be a safe place for their only daughter, who was hell-bent on going to hell.

I was in my early twenties when I drove five hours from the northern suburbs of St. Louis to see Linda Ronstadt in concert with the Eagles and Jackson Browne in Kansas City, Missouri. In performance, Linda Ronstadt had a little bit of a self-conscious air. She didn't move around much, maybe banging a tambourine or snapping her fingers; there was no backdrop of dancers behind her, and harmony vocals were provided by her backup band and sometimes girl singer/songwriters whose songs Linda occasionally recorded and whose careers she thus helped launch—Nicolette Larson, Wendy Waldman, Karla Bonoff. Her stage persona was not a glitzy production but seemed a carefully cultivated performance. This was the tour when Linda wore a Cub Scout uniform on stage. I read reviews that called her a belter, the little lady with the big voice, a rodeo sweetheart, the Queen of Rock . . . How she *looked* was usually a focal point in any review. Of course. It was the seventies, and there were so few solo women in rock, how any woman looked was primary—talent, technique, intelligence were all secondary. A music reviewer for *Rolling Stone* reported, "There is a throbbing edge to Ronstadt's honey-colored soprano that no other singer quite possesses—the edge between vulnerability and willfulness that I find totally, irresistibly sexy." *The edge between vulnerability and willfulness,* a place I longed to visit.

There were two or three guys I talked to about music around this time. Fred was a little guy who lifted weights and had perfect blond bangs and a soft-looking blond beard that he liked to pet. He wrote me long letters quoting Bruce Springsteen song lyrics, but it didn't make me want to listen to Springsteen or pet Fred's beard. Dennis was a guitar freak. He recorded cassette tapes for me of guitarists: Rory Gallagher, Jeff Beck, Eric Clapton and Cream, Jimmy Page. While I could admire the technical proficiency of this music, I didn't know what I was supposed to be feeling as I listened. What I admired most was that Dennis had soft skin like a girl's. Rick and I gave each other the same rock encyclopedias for Christmas, we went to concerts together, and he was the first guy to take me to a motel. At the time, I thought if I sought out relationships with guys I had something in common with, like listening to music, then we would have something to talk about, or I might hear something from them that I hadn't heard before, or I might discover a connection between a shared interest—in music, Mexican food, the Beat poets—that might translate to something more like desire.

In Ronstadt's albums, her song choices, her performance, I found a conduit to my own unruly and unformed emotional landscape. In 1972 rock critic Lester Bangs wrote a version of a rave review of Ronstadt that might be summarized as "she's pretty and so is her voice":

> Her combination of innocence and utter frankness, as well as her disdain for bras and predilection for skimpy blouses tied above her navel, cutoff jeans and being barefoot managed to flip out many a stolid c & w session man. Linda Ronstadt's vocal style is like her physical presence: brimming with passion and vulnerability, tremulous, yet possessed of a core of absolute strength.

At some point I realized I was responding to Linda Ronstadt the same way all those male reviewers were, which made me feel ashamed and so embarrassed that I continued my listening in secret. Never mind sharing, she was mine and mine alone—mine and a few million fans'.

Today, my niece's fifteen-year-old step-daughter can wear a

suit and bring her girlfriend to prom, and every young woman I encounter—my husband's students, the young people I work with—think of their sexual identities as somewhat fluid ("We made out a couple times . . ." "I dated women in college . . ." "I was married for awhile and then we opened up our marriage and I met her and fell in love . . ."). There is trauma and heartbreak always, and such glorious variety of pleasure and romance available to young women.

My parents seemed bewildered by the parade of boys in and out of our house, the cars in the driveway, the ringing phone. Every boy I brought home, who stopped by, or who came over was evaluated by my mother as a potential husband. "What does his father do?" "Where is his family from?" "He looks dirty with that beard." "I don't like you going out with a boy who has his own apartment."

I didn't know how to tell my parents that all the boys were just a wall to prevent any one boy from coming too close. I didn't know how to tell myself that all the boys were a shield so I didn't have to think about what I was thinking about all the time. The first time I had an orgasm with a boy, I cried because I thought it meant I no longer had the excuse of bad sex not to have a boyfriend. Which was the last thing I wanted, except maybe a boyfriend, one boy, who would keep me safe from the other boys. To belong to one man seemed to be the only way a woman might be safe from men in this America.

My parents were so afraid for me. Too afraid to talk to me or listen when I tried to talk to them. During this time, I had a recurring dream that I was being threatened by a sweating, hairy-backed clown, a version of Big Daddy in *Cat on a Hot Tin Roof*, holding me hostage with tradition. My safety was dependent on what I said next, the argument I formed. I had read

somewhere that if you are being attacked, try to make a connection with your attacker. Ask him where he grew up, if he's hungry, tell him he reminds you of your dad, your brother . . . Or
the alternate strategy was to speak up: yell, scream for help, No!
Leave me alone! Stop following me! In the dream, I can't speak—
my mouth is full of dust or glue, and when I try to speak, to
scream, to spit and spit, I can't form words, can't make a sound.
I'm standing still, compliant, waiting for the attack to come; I
could choose to die.

I wanted to talk to my parents, to my mother, who I dis-
trusted and who I wanted to tell everything, but how much
are you supposed to tell someone who loves you with all the
weight and expectation of generations of Italian mothers and
daughters?

I thought I was saying everything by my indifference to
the ten thousand dates with boys; by my hostility toward hope
chests and the celebrity marriages that my girlfriends dissected
like entertainment reporters—the dress, the setting, the helicop-
ters overhead—Farrah Fawcett and Lee Majors, Jessica Lange
and Mikhail Baryshnikov, or Carly Simon and James Taylor; by
the books I left around the house—*Our Bodies, Ourselves, The
Female Eunuch, Against Our Will* by Susan Brownmiller, *Diving into the Wreck*; I didn't know how to articulate what I was
feeling even to myself. I didn't know what I wanted.

You think the love you never had might save you

There was something about a slight woman in an off-the-shoul-
der blouse fronting a band of boys, singing "you got to roll me"

with brass and conviction that left me limp, wilting with . . .
something. What I wanted or who, I had no idea, but I believed
this was a love that could save me.

Like with any great love, longevity meant having the courage
to stay through twists and turns, changes and setbacks. I didn't
have the courage to stay with Linda. I was living on the edge of a
dance floor in a big gay club. I couldn't make sense of my devotion to a rock and roll girl singer. I left her.

Soon after, I left St. Louis with two black trash bags packed
with clothes and a few boxes of books and records, driving a 1976
Chevette that I was still making payments on. I was chasing after
a girl I had met in one of the gay bars in East St. Louis. I had
been plotting my escape from my parents' house in the north
suburbs of St. Louis for years, plotting to escape the seeming
inevitability of hetero marriage and my parents' expectations,
but I had no education, no prospects, and more hair than hope.
I didn't know how to be the agent of my own destiny except
through love. I drove to St. Paul, Minnesota, and moved in with
the girl—a sexy dancing Northwestern Bell repair tech. I cut off
all my hair so nobody would recognize me and became her tenant, subject to cleaning out the refrigerator, wiping up spillovers
on the stove, replacing burned out lightbulbs; at the mercy of
maintenance, repair, and the inevitable eviction. Overwearing
my contact lenses caused corneal abrasions, and until my eyes
healed, I couldn't drive, I couldn't watch TV. I didn't know anybody else in town yet. Sometimes I was in a cloudy room, squint-
ing, all the shapes blurred and indistinct. I didn't own a winter
coat or boots. I didn't know how snow could bury you, how ice
could be invisible, how you could be driving down the street and
suddenly spin out, careening off guardrails into oncoming traffic until a snowbank caught you and you were stopped, stuck,

spring still far away, another soundtrack in another city with another lover.

MY MOTHER AND I SHARE THE SAME FANTASY

I had a fantasy that kept me on the edge of the dance floor. Maybe it was my mother's fantasy. In the fantasy, I move to a big, cold-blooded city east of the Mississippi, like New York or Chicago. I grow out my fingernails. I join a health club. I hire a personal trainer. I drink white wine. I own fine crystal and china. My bra and panties always match. My table settings match. I depilate 80 percent of my body hair. I carry a purse. I buy condoms. I lease a new model Saab. I keep a lavender sachet in my lingerie drawer with my custom-made lingerie.

I am dancing at my brother's wedding, for which I hosted the bridal shower, made the cake, and arranged all three hundred table centerpieces. I'm wearing a royal-blue silk dress, black jet beads and matching earrings. Under my dress, I'm wearing a black silk full slip, a black garter belt, and hose. My dance partner is a beautiful, smooth man wearing an elegant but understated fifteen-million-dollar charcoal-gray pinstripe suit and a white shirt so fine and beautiful you know he bought it from a locked glass display case. He's an international lawyer, or an ex-priest, or an underwear model. Earlier, we posed together in all the family wedding pictures.

Everyone at the wedding is looking at us as we dip and glide across the dance floor. We dance. Old men look at us and weep. Old women sigh. Young men swallow hard and young women lick their lips.

The bass player announces it's time for the bouquet toss. This is the blood sport of weddings. The single women are edgy with wanting or stupefied with self-consciousness. The lesbians in the room are looking everywhere except at each other. In a few years Ellen DeGeneres will come out on a *Time* magazine cover—"Yep, I'm Gay!"—and as a gay character on her sitcom, while Canadian singer k.d. Lang will croon about constant cravings in Western drag or a vest and tie.

There is a long, tense drumroll and a triumphant cymbal crash as the bouquet lands in my open hands, empty no more. Flowers spontaneously spill over my arms, white roses and lilies multiplying, growing like a garden in fast-forward time-lapse photography. It's a blizzard of white, a snowstorm of perfect petals and graceful stems. Flowers wind themselves around the feet of the wedding guests, across the tables and chairs, inching toward the open bar, a heteronormative invasive jungle.

If I didn't hold on to the fantasy that I could stay on the edge of the dance floor, choose to be unqueered as easily as choosing a new dance partner, changing the channel, playing another role, singing a song with hetero-appropriate pronouns, would that mean I was unreservedly gay, unambiguously queer? To be queer was to break my mother's heart.

I carve out a queer life on stage, in film, on vinyl, in blood.

cities and bodies in motion

A house is your third skin, after the skin made of flesh and clothing.
—*Visitation,* Jenny Erpenbeck

where we started

We met on the hottest day of the year. Mutual friends living in a third-floor apartment without air conditioning cooked a spicy soup and invited us to dinner. At that table we had nothing in common except our glistening faces, our fevered tongues, our longing for one crisp, cool lettuce leaf. P—— was not age appropriate, which means she was too young in that way of being too unwounded by the world. I was well-worn, paying legal fees to extricate myself from a relationship that included joint property, and she was living like an intellectual primitive or a teenage boy who didn't wear underwear, subsisting on frozen waffles and Raisin Bran. I was a Full. Grown. Woman. I could kick down a door, shoot a gun, break the neck of a chicken with my bare hands, and make a good Act of Contrition before breakfast. I was thinking of making a move, although at the time I wasn't sure if the move meant taking off her pants or getting out of town. Maybe a dose of the geographic cure would fix my accumulating impatience with Minnesota: the tight-hipped, blank-faced locals; the work of endless winters—bundle up, scrape, shovel, defrost, thaw, repeat; bodies buried in big boots and multiple layers. In Minnesota I was my own Italian American essential-

ized cliché. I grew basil. I had a garden Madonna. I threatened
to cut my enemies. I had too much hair. I yelled. Minnesotans
backed away blinking. She moved forward to meet me. A bathroom with plastic tiles and curling linoleum came between us.
Make a new bathroom and I will leave my toothbrush here, I
said. I moved in, bringing my fat old orange-and-white cat, the
companion of my youth, my religion, heartfriend.

POSSIBLE CITY: MOVING WHILE STANDING STILL

*There was a family that built a four-bedroom house in South-
ern Illinois. Then they moved to a suburb outside of Minneapolis and replicated the Illinois house, down to the wallpaper,
carpet, window treatments, and paint choices. They lived in
the duplicated house for twenty-five years, raised a family, and
then imagined a third house, just like the old houses. But better. The second house was jacked up and moved down the road,
and the first generation rebuilt the original house in the spot
where the second house had stood. The family lived in the same
house in two different structures within walking distance of
each other. The children grew up in the second house and then
an adult daughter and her husband moved into the duplicated
third house, just exchanging the daughter's childhood bedroom
for the bedroom that had been her parents'. The family didn't
have to move on or move past or imagine a future in different
rooms. They lived in their shared past and never left home.*

CALLING YOU INTO VIEW

"The blue or gray?" Every day you ask for my opinion on your outfit, whether you are going to work or to work out, or you ask about some item of men's clothing in your online shopping cart. A preoccupation with men's fashion is not new to you, and inserting myself into dressing you is not new for me. Over the past twenty years, nothing in the material world has mattered more to you than what you wear. Early in our relationship when you were still shopping at discount stores, paying off student loans, rolling up the legs of too-long pants, wearing baggy T-shirts, I blindfolded you and brought you to a tailor in Minneapolis to have three shirts made as a birthday surprise.

When three shirts are the extent of your dress wardrobe, you have to resist the urge for the bold and bright, which create too much of a signature look and are too well remembered. Three shirts are more versatile if they are less notable. A narrow stripe, an end-on-end weave, a pinpoint Oxford. The first rendering of the shirts included feminine darts and a straight hemline. You wouldn't come out of the fitting room. "This is a girl's shirt," you said despairingly, plucking the shirt away from your body. No detail of construction or quality of fabric would soothe you. A clarifying conversation with the tailor about a more masculine fit, and he agreed to remake the shirts. "The most important thing is that you leave here happy," he said. We were hopeful at the time that new shirts would do the trick.

I wore a pair of black boots, a sleeveless shirt, worn jeans. I trusted I looked good. It was the clearest thing I knew about myself from about age fifteen on. I was strong-featured (a.k.a. ethnic exotic) and curvy, with a narrow waist and child-bearing hips that had borne no children. In the Land of Ten Thousand Blondes, people were afraid of my hair. I wore oversized tops, sweater layers, black dresses with scarves, boots of every color. I thought I was much bigger than I actually was, a big'un, sprawling flesh, out of frame, and often I was dressing to cover up or to hide myself. Maybe because you were so petite next to me, *wiry* the adjective most often used to describe you. I bought a dog-walking winter coat in a Large, anticipating wearing multiple layers underneath. The coat was so big it was like wearing a sleeping bag.

You looked like a femme Johnny Depp at this stage—tattoos, streaked hair, big black boots, tank tops, eyeglasses as art objects. We were living in Minneapolis. We had been together ten years. This was the period of vests—you wore striped vests, brocade vests, a beautiful navy vest with a silk lining striped blue and white peeking out from the lapels.

minneapolis, city of the upper middle west: carrying rocks to chicago

In the grip of weariness, my mother newly dead, no longer able to bear our comfortable and convenient life in the corner-lot four-square house with cedar fencing or our life of daily walks along the Mississippi River in the city of the Upper Middle West; no longer able to bear all those backyard parties with neighborly neighbors and the good, open-mouthed laughing dogs; no longer able to bear the straight-line progression to paid-off mortgages toward one-level retirement living, we said goodbye to our easy queer youth, the chorus of ex-lovers and bar and bedroom dramas, and moved to the next city which was there waiting for us— Chicago—the City of the Middle West.

I sort and consider. P—— pitches and throws. Her inclination is to start over, leave behind her high school basketball and tennis trophies, recycle all the iterations of her dissertation. She shakes her head and sighs at my boxes of journals, the planner calendars I keep in case I have to look back at meetings I went to or due dates I missed over the years. Whatever we put in the alley—the futon frame, mismatched dishes, a rusty cast iron fry pan—disappears overnight. I anticipate regret for pages discarded, because everything is material in a writer's life—my life—all the stories: handwritten drafts, timesheets from a job I held for nine months, a file of winter and spring solstice cards from Emilie Autumn, each featuring a portrait of her and a series of lop-eared rabbits—all of them named Ezekiel, all wearing seasonally appropriate matching outfits. Are the rabbit portraits a writing prompt for a story I will write in the future about a woman and her rabbits?

I believe in *garden* as a way of life, like writing perhaps, as a way to make order, create a point of view, find one's place in the world. I can make a garden anywhere, but who will love the cream-colored limestone sills I gathered from the stone yard picking lot, the flagstone path to the buckeye tree, the fussy, extravagant irises, and yellow floribunda roses? I make a landscape map of the gardens to leave with the buyers of the house. We hear from our realtor that the buyer's interest in our house was based on their perspective that everything was already "done." But a garden doesn't maintain itself. The Niobe clematis will flower on new growth on old stems, but the *Clematis tangutica* requires hard pruning. Shortly before we move, I dig up the pink floribunda rose named after a textile artist and a Japanese painted fern to give to a friend. P—— tells me I am jeopardizing the sale of the house—everything inside and outside of the house now belongs to the new owner. I fill in the holes I leave, camouflage the empty spaces with mulch. A red Buddha is stolen from our front porch, another hole.

I pull a few granite boulders from the yard and tie together leftover cedar fence planks to move with us to Chicago. I will build a raised bed, and besides, I had paid for those rocks—including delivery—I had lifted and moved them all over the Minneapolis yard. I had paid for those rocks in every way.

I carried rocks to Chicago, to our tiny pocket backyard, like a memento mori of a past life. Before we left, P— added to her collection of tattoos with an image on her shin of two frogs jumping out of water. We were the frogs. I quit my job, casting off dental insurance and 401(k) contributions. We were taking a leap.

POSSIBLE CITY: IN THE WHITE SPACE

At Abiquiu, P— and I visit Georgia O'Keeffe's open studio overlooking the red clay mountains beneath the blue skies of New Mexico. The walls are white, the kitchen, the sheets on her narrow bed—white. O'Keeffe lived without clutter or things; a ledge of stones and bleached bones, music in the evening, a garden outside her door, both enclosed and open. The walled garden protected tender crops and extended the growing season. Sometimes all we want is to rest in the white space, inhabit the white light, stand in the doorway she loved to paint. O'Keeffe's husband never visited the light of New Mexico.

chicago, city of the middle west: where the chickens come home to roost

You can find us in the orange brick bungalow with the pocket backyard in the far North Side neighborhood. The house has an inoperable fireplace that had been staged for the showing with a charred log and a pile of ashes in the fire box. Storm windows are bolted in place like armor defending the passage of light and air. The house feels so heavy and dark I can barely stand upright. In daylight, with the original dining room light fixtures on, I need a flashlight to find my way through the gloom of dark wood-work and dirty windows. I miss my dead mother, I carry her dissatisfaction, her fear of open garage doors and public rest-rooms. I miss my fat old orange-and-white cat who doesn't live to make the move, whose name spells out my password on all my accounts. There is a fog of grief that I vacuum up every day. For a while I think the fog is in the city, in the house, but the fog is in me. There we take up new routines, new dog-walking routes, new modes of transportation, new house projects.

CALLING YOU INTO VIEW

At different times during our relationship, I joked with you that we didn't go together. It was a joke and it was also true. While other couples might dress to complement one another on special occasions—parties, weddings, gallery openings—his tie picking up a color in her dress, her and her sweatshirts, or the gay male couple with corresponding facial hair, most often if we were out together, our outfits were completely unrelated.

I shopped alone, like most women past forty, fifty, appalled by and despairing of my reflection in the cruel dressing room mirrors, slapping my hips as if that would reduce their size on the spot, or buying multiple sizes and colors to try on at home before returning everything. Terror is a condition of the female body—How am I seen? Who sees me? What do I look like?—a

condition that you inhabit in ways I acknowledge I don't understand. I didn't understand what it meant to you, in all your tattoos and your shape-shifting wardrobe, to insist on *not* being
seen as a woman in woman's clothes.

CALLING YOU INTO VIEW

This was the period of injuries by shapewear: a sprained thumb,
a bruised rib. Every time I wore shapewear, I peed on my hands
trying to move aside a stretchy fabric panel over the toilet. More
than once following an evening at the theater, a little tipsy, looking forward to taking off my eye makeup, I scissored myself out
of a pricey body shaper that clung too insistently. At your brother's wedding, you wore an exquisitely tailored vest, gray wool
flannel trousers, a tie with a Windsor knot. I wore a taupe pencil
skirt with a matching sweater set. I expected that five years from
then, when your brother and his wife looked at their wedding
photos, they would wonder who the woman was standing next
to you in all the pictures. I had no faith that we would land on
corresponding styles, that we would ever go together. You were
so restless, your style chronically shifting, the only constant the
ascending price point. Your look was about you and how you
wanted to be seen.

  We came to Chicago together, but we are not in the same
place. My view from every window is a brick wall of another
building, a line of parked cars. I see car crashes and murder out
the windows. I keep looking.

"You are seduced by the surface," I say accusingly, feeling our age difference becoming more pronounced between us, my seductive surface eroding. "I see what could be."

"You see the one green leaf in the burnt out forest," P—— says. She wanted a house that was fully formed, that her restless intellect could move in and inhabit, a house that didn't require remaking. I wanted a house that contained possibility, that I could shape to our living, a love that was smooth and free from wrinkles, nourished by expensive aesthetic maintenance, like my skin, my hair, my exterior.

"Where do you want to live?" P—— asks me. Not here. Anywhere but here. It was her job we followed to Chicago, which made everything her fault.

Our first fall in the neighborhood of West Rogers Park, I built a path from the garage with a carload of Chicago common brick I bought on Craigslist. A neighbor offered an overflow pallet of red rocks to make a dry-stack flower bed wall. Something in the heft and weight of solid surfaces began to ground me in this new city. In a community yoga class during shavasana, I smelled the smoke of my dead mother's cigarette. I was both comforted and crowded by the fact that she had followed me to this new city. There were two back doors to our bungalow that opened to an oversized deck. We had a window installed in place of one of the redundant doors. The contractor showed me the small openings in the brick above the window flashing that allowed water to drain—the weep holes.

By spring I was in a different place. I could go but not back. Nobody returns to where they've been. I don't get Mississippi bluffs along Lake Street in Minneapolis, the groomed bike trails, the good dogs trotting obediently at heel on loose leashes, their rapt faces upturned toward what they love best—*you only you,* the dogs pant. I see the scrappy crabapple and dogwood trees soon to burst into bloom in Warren Park, mud splashing on the dogs' legs, all the children running. I walked away from where we were. I trusted the motion, which implies faith in what comes next.

When the fog finally clears, I walk the city, go into every building. Everywhere I look, I am happy for what I see. Look! There and there! There are stories everywhere in Chicago:

One of the stories is about the schoolteacher who lived in our bungalow all of her life. The schoolteacher's parents bought the house in 1927 from the architect who designed it. Every detail, from the wallpaper to the matching brass sconces in the living room to the color of the paint on the moldings, was specified in the home's original blueprints. Before we replace and add on, I want to know what was here before.

I join the cult of bungalow owners. We talk for hours about restoration of wood windows, antique door hardware; I learn the language of finishes and patina: gloss, semigloss, satin, matte.

POSSIBLE CITY: LONG LEAF PINE BONES

My Texan writer friend has a story house in Taos. The items in the house—the 18-lite door with a saint painted on every glass panel, the blue kachina doll with the blond braids, the chair altars—have been collected over years. Every object, every construction detail has a story. There is also the story behind the stories: the wide floorboards had been pulled from New Orleans shotgun houses that were being torn down to make room for

*an Albertson's grocery store and then stored in a warehouse
in Alabama. They are longleaf pine at least a hundred years
old, dented, scarred. Many of the wide boards were painted
at some iteration of their life cycle—green, orange, blue, tur-
quoise. The boards traveled on a truck from Birmingham
across the country. Square-headed nails were removed and
the boards installed in an adobe house in the Southwest, where
next they were hand-sanded, so just traces of paint remained,
and, finally, milk-washed. Removed from their origin in the
pine forests of Mississippi, a flooded cottage in New Orleans,
the labor that cut the trees, milled the planks is hidden. Where
walls go up and come down, and people enter, make a home,
and exit, now the floor supports three generations of a Texas
family and has hosted at least one wedding, numerous dinner
parties, the toenail-clicking passage of several dogs, dancing,
all the dancing, the floors, the bones of the house, white as ash.*

We have different friends in Chicago, different from our same-
sex couple, ex-lover-potential-new-lover friends in Minneapolis;
our dinner parties are configured differently. We are the lesbian
hosts to the smarty arty crowd, to our bungalow neighbors. At
the table, our guests talk all at once, they eat and drink everything and are still hungry, have more to say. We go to BYOB
restaurants and carry bottles with screw caps so we don't have
to pay an uncorking fee. We open windows, add doors, rebuild
sidewalls, match old and new bricks, old and new mortar. I keep
chickens, collect eggs, pink and green and brown, a year-round
Easter palette in the glorious gray city with the pink and gold
buildings on the lake where the Chicago River flows backward.

boston, the gateway to new england: where nobody knows our names

Then another move. We cast off our heavy, oversized, overstuffed oak furniture, furniture made for generations of sprawling and stretching, furniture that had assumed the shape of our lives. We acquire a slim couch, a chair, both trim and streamlined so they can be moved up the narrow stairs to our middle apartment in a ubiquitous Boston triple decker in Savin Hill. We are living nimble, renting. I spend the winter emptying shelves, transferring all our music CDs to a computer. Then I forget the point and pack the ripped CDs into boxes and carry them to the basement. I work with young people, so young they eat air, they own nothing. I give them things, feed them.

I become a balcony gardener, pots planted with kitchen herbs, baskets of impatiens and begonias; something trailing, something climbing, the teak Adirondack chairs that moved with us from Minneapolis, the wrought iron table. The third-floor tenants with no shade protection above their balcony grow tomatoes in pots. The balconies of the three apartments are stacked on top of one another; below is a driveway, and there are trees in our view.

I am always walking uphill or downhill, my knees aching, the dogs pull and pull at the end of their leashes but cannot pull me into this new city, our new life. As P—— rides her bike through traffic, along the water, she tracks the miles, adding them up like money in the bank. The jumping licking panting dog loses the use of her back legs. P—— has shoulder surgery, knee surgery, then top surgery, then another knee surgery. We are all limping. I meet a Minnesota transplant. I think we will become friends over traffic and the cost of real estate. But we don't. I don't know how to enter this city. People have always liked me—not these people. I think I will go to sea, become beachy and boaty, but the beach is crowded with cottages and campfires, so many rocks and broken shells.

We move again to a cement box in Southie with a water view. We are down a dog. We are down, although we now live on the top floor. There are no storytelling details in the latest new place—there is no history. Everything is MDF and granite, there is no surface I want to run my hands over, the water-view windows don't open. P——changes her pronouns, changes her name, although the first letter of her name and his name remain the same. Everything changes. We don't know anybody who owns their own home in Boston. A few people we meet own a house outside of the city where it is too far to get to without a car.

POSSIBLE CITY: PUTTING DOWN ROOTS

On a hike in the Madonie region of Sicily, Mario our guide leads us up winding dirt roads to a hilltop where he harvests manna every summer from the ash trees growing there. There are olive trees, antique varieties, that only grow on these cliffs. Nearby is a one-room round structure with stone walls and a thatch roof with a skylight. Mario has installed built-in cupboards and shelving in the structure. He calls it his retreat. He will soon move two sheep to the hill to graze down the brush. He grafts almond trees, presses olives to extract the pale golden oil smelling of grass and pepper. The wind blows, the sun is so bright. There is a raised platform suspended between trees where he sometimes sleeps. He once wandered the steep streets of San Francisco, a worker in a restaurant. He is tall and slim, and he

*moves with precision and delicacy. Following him, I see beech
branches spread across his shoulders like wings, while around
his hat, stems of pink and white orchids twine. With every step,
his roots sink deep.*

marriage: city of shifting identities

In the grip of weariness, no longer able to bear her cumbersome
girlhood, on the verge of middle age, P——transitions from queer
female to man—not trans man, not nonbinary, not queer—but
man, dude, bro, brutha man. Through the baptism of hormones,
P——is born again a guy, a member of the snapback-hat sneaker
culture tribe in the City of Testosterone.

CALLING YOU INTO VIEW

From Minneapolis to Chicago to Boston, you were the girl in
tank tops with tats, the girl in the corduroy pants and vests, the
girl in the custom-tailored shirts with the buttons on the right,
front placket, president spread collar—that boyish queer girl, the
one who disappeared, your body your own, taking my lover, my
beloved with you.

   As you went away, I went along. There is no place in a lesbian
marriage to say I don't know you now that you are a man. When
it comes to gender transition, you're either on the trans train or
you're transphobic. But I don't recognize you with that haircut,
that beard. I don't know you as he and him. How were you always
a man? If you were, how did I not know? Did I ever know you?
What happened to her, that person I thought I knew and loved?

I always thought I was the most loyal, the fiercest of lovers. With no imagination whatsoever, I imagined my husband doing things that men do to women who love them: leave, cheat with younger women, drag them across the country, let them fall in love with a light fixture or a built-in birch buffet with prairie glass doors and then dump the old wives and girlfriends on the side of the road. I felt homeless, cast off, already abandoned and alone.

It is always Thanksgiving with opposing viewpoints at the dinner table in our new house in Boston, but the lines are drawn along gender not politics. Is this our marriage?

When we moved to Massachusetts, gay marriage was already legal, which was why we had married in Boston in 2012. P—— had the job with benefits, and if we were married, I could be on her health insurance and privy to all the other perks of married life, which I hoped to discover. I expected that with marriage, our relationship—already good in a way that years together create a shared life with merged bookshelves and a mortgage— would get better. I did not expect four years into our marriage to be married to a man, this as a presidential candidate stalked a woman, his opponent, in a public debate, hissed *nasty*; as another man cried like a crying baby as another woman spoke about his unspeakable acts of intimidation and assault perpetrated against her.

Marriage benefits did not mean that we could afford to live in Boston. Priced out of two Boston apartments, exhausted from putting our things in boxes and taking them out in another new space, we moved again, buying a condo in a two-family unit in Jamaica Plain. P—— is a man in Boston, in our new home, but I can't locate myself in this new relationship configuration.

DISAPPEARING FROM VIEW

I feel like a 1950s housewife wearing an apron standing at the stove, dressing and undressing behind a coyly half-closed door. It's easy sometimes to hate myself as much as the world hates older women. No amount of breathe-in-love, breathe-out-love toxic positivity, nor two glasses of wine at dinner can reassure me. Every couple with a cisgender female partner in a relationship with a masculine-identifying trans person I stalk on social media consists of a hot young trans guy with a hot young cis girl. They look good together. This is not my lesbian marriage.

He is who he always wanted to be. In the city we have come to of white men split along the disaster in the White House in 2018, along our borders, in our streets and our humanity, divided into my loved ones and those that would deport, arrest, shoot in the streets those I love. In the disaster that is America, in the City of Testosterone, our foundation is cracked, load-bearing walls won't hold, floors buckle, windows fall out of frame.

CALLING US INTO VIEW

You might wear a green leather motorcycle jacket that you found at a vintage store and a newsboy cap. I'd have on a red red red two-piece dress with a ruffle skirt that knocked them all dead dead dead.

He would love to move again to where we've never been before, where no one remembers his previous pronouns. I thought we were living with everything—real estate stories, parking, all the dogs. Were we careless with what we had made, did we have so much, had we traveled so far that we could leave it, expecting there would be still more? What would *more* look like? We've always moved together, following his career, my devotion to gardening.

Do I want to build the same house over and over, drag our queer couple traditions with us everywhere we go—I make a new garden in a new growing zone, Carl gets a new tattoo. I toss old spices and opened condiments, restocking the kitchens, embarking on another search in a new city for the hot Italian sausage that is not too porky, too coarse, or too chewy. Do I want to live with the same floor plan in a museum of our former selves?

Do I want my own private white space in a landlocked desert? A resting place, a laundromat where there are no machines out of order and I can sit with a cup full of quarters and bleach the stains of dirty living. No husband but light.

Or will I live in a customized revision, a haunted history of material and texture and color, built in the memory of her and me.

Perhaps I will walk ahead alone into a space I cultivate, only dirt, only garden, a life among the vegetables.

I know how to move, how to discard and declutter, sort and pack. I also know how to move on, how to leave things behind and decide what things to carry with us. I drive around this hard city of cobblestones, of granite. I can create landscapes wherever we go, but I don't have a vision of this place where we have arrived. What is the new city waiting for us? Will we each go our own way to our own new city, or will our lives be renewed as we shelter together?

Our ephemeral, transitory bodies replace 330 billion cells daily. Every eighty to one hundred days, 30 trillion cells are replenished—the equivalent of a new me or a new you. We all transition. In one way or another. I would like to go back to where we were, but nobody gets to stay the same. I'm so much older now than that young, queer, femme lesbian in the sleeveless top, the dangerous shapewear, the red ruffle dress. I know what was here before age's humiliation, which doesn't stop me from being scared that my life will suffer a dramatic, sudden change. Which it has, which it will again.

"We have love over time and place," my husband says to me. "We're still us." That's not nothing. That's a marriage.

Among the men I hate—the men who don't listen; the men who mock a woman's terror, the echo of their laughter in all the rooms; the men I cross the street, step off the sidewalk to avoid— can I learn to love a man now? A new man in selvedge denim and Japanese shashiko, with Timberlands and a swagger, who I see in my garden, who makes a new place for himself in the world where we live.

the burning bed

Longing is our legacy. To be a third-generation Sicilian woman in America is to live with loss and disconnection. We are born to blood and shame and rage. Well, at least in my family we are.

Traveling in Sicily in 2019 with friends, I saw what looked to be the effects of time or perhaps an earthquake in a piazza in the town of Castelbuono in the Madonie Mountains: a crumbling fourteenth-century stone fountain, a one-handed clockface, a headless statue. "We are here to find out where the grief began," said my friend Mary.

*

I was my mother's greatest shame: the perfect daughter who broke her mother's heart by sleeping with girls, so no matter what else I was, what else I did—graduate from college when I was thirty-five, plan my parents' fiftieth wedding anniversary, call every day—I was first and always a profound disappointment and embarrassment to my small Sicilian mother who was bigger than any New World.

*

2018. I was bleeding. I must have forgotten to replace my weekly estrogen patch, which had happened before, or maybe I had skipped one or two of the daily orange progesterone pills. I had been on hormone replacement therapy for several years, the only thing that helped with the hot flash symptoms and sleeplessness. It was a convenient and easy accommodation to the inconvenient and debilitating symptoms of menopause. Forgetting to replace the estrogen patch or missing a few doses of progesterone might result in breakthrough bleeding. So although I hadn't had a period in ten years, I didn't think too much about it, except we were supposed to leave Boston in the fall to live in Berlin for four months. My husband had been awarded a fellowship, and the plan was that I would accompany him to Germany—if we were getting along, if we were still married, if we didn't blow each other up before then. It was March now and I was bleeding. I had already found a dog/house sitter, scheduled vet appointments for both dogs, lined up a weekly cleaner for the months we would be gone, put dog food delivery on an automatic schedule, and set up appointments with my dentist and optometrist. I didn't want to be in a foreign country and need a cavity filled or new glasses. I'd add a pap smear to the list and check it off. A pap smear led to an ultrasound, which led to an endometrial biopsy. It was July now and I had been diagnosed with cancer.

the bombed out fountain

I am angry nearly every day of my life.
—Marmee from *Little Women*, Louisa May Alcott

She was so angry all the time. She was angry when she cleaned, when she dusted and vacuumed, when she folded laundry—she squared corners and flattened wrinkles, her hands like bricks. She was angry grocery shopping, angry when it rained, when it stopped raining. She was angry at stoplights, waiting to make a left turn, angry looking for parking, paying for parking. She was angry waking in the morning and angry before she fell asleep at night; all the weather in her dreams was bad.

the mother's regret

I knew what I was. I knew who I was. I knew where I came from. I believed my life would be beautiful, that I would know great joy and always feel loved. How could I know that my only daughter, who was born to beauty and talent, a perpetual fountain, would become a scene of ruin?

*

On display at the Warren Anatomical Museum at Harvard is a skull with a hole through the left cheek and another hole at the top of the skull. This is the skull of Phineas Gage. In 1848 Gage was working on a railroad in Vermont, using a three-foot-seven-inch-long iron bar to tamp down a powder charge. The charge detonated prematurely, and the tamping iron was projected into Gage's left cheek and exited the top of this head, landing about thirty yards behind him. He survived, but according to some accounts, he suffered a dramatic character change. He went from being competent and well-liked to being, as described by his doctor, "fitful, irreverent, and grossly profane, showing little deference for his fellows." Gage's skull on display revealed the wounds made by the iron bar, traumatic holes in and out, a rage that entered and exited, that changed Gage's personality.

"If you're going to have cancer, this is the best kind of cancer to have," said my smooth-faced surgeon, who was not the woman gynecologist who had diagnosed me and told me at the ultrasound that she didn't want to wait to do a biopsy, that if I was up for it, she recommended getting it done at the same time. I took the gynecologist's call as I was driving south on the Jamaica-way, the four-lane parkway designed by Frederick Law Olmsted, part of the Emerald Necklace of green spaces, a winding, narrow roadway that seemed to attract many of the worst drivers in Boston. I don't remember that the efficient doctor said "cancer" on the phone. I think she said that the biopsy had come back positive and the next step would be to refer me to a gynecologic oncologist. That was the meeting with the surgeon whose face was so dewy and soft-looking he looked suspended in time, ageless from the neck up.

Healthcare in Boston is world-class, and I had a first-rate care team. The surgery date had been accelerated to try and accommodate timing so I could accompany my husband to Germany. "Cut and done" was the treatment recommendation, a laparoscopic hysterectomy and a biopsy of lymph nodes. If the cancer was contained to the uterus, barring complications, I'd be cleared for travel in three weeks, although full recovery would take several more weeks or longer.

The smooth-faced surgeon met with me and my husband in his office. There was a discussion about the surgery: a few small incisions, minimal scarring, limited discomfort, expected full recovery. The surgeon was reasonable, reassuring without warmth, like a car mechanic. In Mount Vernon, New York, there is an auto repair business called Surgical Car Repair. Their tagline is "Are you looking for a car repair technician that is as meticulous as a surgeon?" In this case, was my body the car? I'm not sure.

Cancer is a disease that lends itself to metaphor, maybe because we don't want to hear what it *is*—abnormal cells multiplying, forming tumors, sometimes spreading, sometimes killing you. We can only bear to hear what it is *like*—a battle, a war, a journey, the body a well-functioning car, in my case, with a little rust, high mileage, wear and tear on the tires, in need of a repair technician with a perfect manicure.

At some point in the meeting with the surgeon, I stopped listening. This was not owing to a barrage of medical terminology or overwhelming details; my attention was caught, fixated on my husband's shoes. He was wearing a new pair of sneakers, although all his sneakers were new, most of them acquired during the year of his gender transition. The sneakers were so vividly orange they blocked the sun. I couldn't see anything else. His orange sneakers sucked up all the air in the doctor's office so I couldn't react or respond. I was being suffocated by orange sneakers.

the one-handed clockface

Rage became a layer of my skin.
—*Rage Becomes Her: The Power of Women's Anger*, Soraya Chemaly

She was at a level of rage that was incendiary. "I can't get a grip," she said to her friends, her therapist. "I feel like I'm living in a frat house." The husband set an alarm to wake up in the middle of the night to bid on newly released sneakers. Shoe boxes showed up at the door weekly, sometimes daily. Every pair of shoes had to be modeled with appropriate athletic wear or jeans and T-shirts and baseball caps. *Do you like the yellow? Can I roll the cuffs?* He was going through a delayed boyhood, and she was a few years away from collecting social security. She had no opinions as to the red-and-black high-tops versus the camouflage mesh or the triple black versus the butter color, except the butter looked like raw dough. She matched his spending on sneakers by donating money to food banks and to legal services for immigrants and gun control. She burned and burned and burned about the injustices of the world and blamed it all on sneaker culture.

*

My mother was a very small person, but she took up all the space in the universe. In physical space, my mother and I had lived six hundred miles apart, but our blood curdled in each other's veins, our breath pushed against each other. We were not good together and we were the same apart. We had lived at a distance for years and years, and still we crowded one another.

the mother's regret

I stayed with your father for you children, so you could have everything I wouldn't be able to give you on my own. Marriage is what women do, what we have to do. Your father was not a bad man, but he promised me so much more. He was weak. I wanted more for my children. Grandma told me my place is with my husband, so I stayed. You should stay too.

*

While I was waiting for the date of my surgery to be confirmed, my husband's brother and nephew came to Boston from Minneapolis to do a round of college visits. I adored my brother-in-law and the nephew, but this time I couldn't be in the same room with them. Over the course of the visit, they sprawled in front of the TV, binge-watching James Bond movies and eating delivery pizza and wings. I violated my highest value of hospitality and would not cook for them, putting out boxes of cereal in the morning right in front of my husband's disbelieving face, claiming I had forgotten to buy eggs. "Sorry, it's all we have." I felt overrun by men in the house and filled with hate. I wanted a sweet-faced girl to make me a cup of tea, rub my feet, to serve me. The flip-flops the nephew wore smelled like adolescent vitality and thoughtlessness. The smell made me feel more sick than I already was.

"You can't talk to a man about this," my friends told me. Dianne's husband went to work the day after her hysterectomy. He left her at home alone with three dogs. Mia's husband didn't even go with her to the surgery.

Another friend who had survived breast cancer called me from Paris. "A man is never going to understand what you're going through, even a man with a vag. You can't make yourself that vulnerable to a man. Don't do it."

I had lived forty years in the community and embrace of women, my lovers and friends and closest connections, and now of all the confusing and frustrating aspects of my husband's gender transition, I didn't understand this clear demarcation of subjects that could not be addressed between us. There was something about losing my uterus that was inappropriate to share with the person closest to me, *because* that person was a man. When had we reached the limits of what was possible to know between us? We both knew firsthand what men were capable of, and I thought we had each made a choice to choose women.

At a time when I was desperately needy for reassurance and comfort, my husband doubled down on the notion that I had abandoned him through his transition, and we became pitted against each other. "You're lucky," he said to me. "All your friends are texting and sending gifts and cards, unequivocally supporting you. You know who has been there for me in my transition? Let's see, Dr. Scott, who hooks me up with T. Leann, of course," referring to his $200-an-hour therapist who he sometimes saw several times a week, "my swim coach, my brothers when they can take time to look up from their own lives to notice me, but not my judging friends who judge me, not my life partner. Not my wife. Not you."

I couldn't grasp that his transition was not something he was doing to us, to me. I had done what I could do, going through the motions, begrudgingly, like my home was being remodeled to someone else's taste while I was clinging to the shell of the old house. His friend, Lee, who had transitioned twelve years earlier when he was single, had flown to Florida from NYC to have a double mastectomy and recuperated alone in a hotel room with room service and a private nurse. At least I had been there through my husband's top surgery and recovery. He hadn't been alone, but as he told me more than once, he had felt completely alone.

And now he was just finding his body as I felt I was losing mine.

the headless statue

She thought the cancer had taken over her personality, a hot spike through her skull that made her irritable and impatient, filled with unending rage. When the eight-year-old boy next door and his dog were in the yard ignoring her hand-lettered sign that said "Give Plants a Chance," stepping over the garden pot barricades and wire fence she had carefully arranged, trampling her painstakingly tended Solomon's seal and ferns, she forgot he was a kid who didn't have one thought for her precious plants, and she popped out the backdoor yelling, her head on fire.

*

In my family there was always an implied blame if anybody got sick, especially with cancer. Nobody ever said the word "cancer," like the word itself was infected, but the insinuation was that cancer implied "bad blood" or a character defect. In obituaries, the word "cancer" never appeared. It was "died after a long illness." My mother was the quickest to lay blame for illness, although she smoked for years and years when we all knew smoking was linked to lung cancer. Then she sneak-smoked, hiding her cigarettes and lighter under the dish towels in the kitchen so she wouldn't risk being banned from babysitting the grandkids, her sons insisting on a smoke-free environment for their offspring. When I visited, she smoked at the kitchen table, nothing to hide.

Lung cancer is an ugly way to die, I said to her, like mother like daughter. So is being alone and unloved, she said.

the mother's regret

Children are God's blessing. Your own children. Blood of your blood. Bone of your own. On the news, five girls, just out of high school, were killed in a car accident when they drove into a trac-tor trailer truck, the driver decapitated. They were cheerleaders, from western New York, beautiful girls with their whole lives ahead of them. There were nine eyewitnesses to the crash. The driver did not apply her brakes. That is my fear for you, that you are driving toward a tractor trailer truck, all your girlfriends in the car with you, no brakes.

*

I couldn't put a first-person possessive pronoun in front of the word cancer and say "my." The cancer was an uninvited, unwel-come interloper. *She* had cancer. *She* had succumbed to illness, had followed her husband's career around like a shadow, had left jobs and benefits packages and moved away from communities and friends she loved. Early in 2018, the cancer year, I left the job where I had worked for eight years. It was a job working with a group of young people that I loved who all worked for my hus-band, which meant I did too. It was time. I could start collecting a pension from the big fat corporate job. Since the diagnosis, I had seen an expression pass over my husband's face, and I was sure it was something like repugnance—toward my age, this ill-ness, my need.

We tell ourselves a story when we are angry, and every story can burn down a world.

In the mid-eighties, self-help guru Louise Hay was a leader in the power of positive thinking movement, "change your thinking, change your life." The book she wrote about how to heal physical illnesses, including her own cervical cancer, by using positive thought along with forgiveness and overcoming despair sold fifty million copies and launched a New Age publishing empire. In the Hay model, cancer was caused by resentment and anger, and the patient owned the blame. A contemporary homeopathic healer and Hays follower claims, "Cancer is a byproduct of tremendous anger either expressed or suppressed. . . . The body, like everything else in our life is a mirror of our inner thoughts—it is always talking to us. We must listen to it."

What was my body saying?

Since the 2016 presidential election, all I had heard loud and clear was that I was in danger. My loved ones were in danger. There was no safe place for women, people of color, queer people, or immigrants, not in the country where I lived, nor in a marriage to a man. Since the 2016 presidential election, all men were culpable, every day was another panic attack, another PTSD response, pulse quickening, a pressure in my chest, a bolt through my head. After the 2016 election, all the women I knew walked hunched and hurrying, car keys threaded through their fingers, ready to be used as a weapon. I went to bed with headphones on. I didn't trust myself in the company of my own thoughts. A man in my bed, an abuser in the White House. I felt some version of sheltered white liberal shock that made me hold tight to handrails, avoid open flames, expecting to trip headfirst down a flight of stairs at any moment, the long fall to the bottom.

break the glass

Anger travels through me, pushes aside everything else in my heart,
pouring up the vents.
Every night I wake to this anger
—"The Glass Essay," Anne Carson

In the 1890s, Mary Sweeney, from Black River Falls, Wisconsin,
was prone to "mania" that she treated with cocaine, and when
she was coked up, she'd go out and smash windows. Mary rode
the train from St. Paul, Minnesota, to Milwaukee, La Crosse, Eau
Claire, Madison, and everywhere she traveled, she left a trail of
broken glass. She'd go on a smashing spree, get locked up in
jail or the Wisconsin Hospital for the Insane, and come down.
Then she'd get out, get high again, and get back on the train
looking for new glass frontiers. Broken windows became her
signature. It was reported that "she appear[ed] to be perfectly
rational on all subjects except that of window smashing." Why
windows? Why not barn burning or rock chucking or a spray
of bullets? Was it the satisfying sound of glass shattering? That
gratifying, nonlethal punctuation when other forms of expression are insufficient, when you have reached the end of civilized
communication?

I thought of myself as sturdy. I tolerated discomfort well—I
was able to work in corporate settings for years and years, long
enough to become vested and accumulate a pension—I was not
prone to headaches or falls, I didn't often get colds. I'd never had
a surgery before the hysterectomy. My body was a good dancer,
reliable, able to take me reasonable distances. In the face of
the ailments of others, I have referred to myself as "arrogantly

healthy," and I have also thought, secretly, judgmentally, like mother like daughter, "you reap what you sow."

The body that I had carried around for so long, clothed and sheltered, fed and overfed, had so much fun with, pushed and stretched, had betrayed me. The fucker. I could have stabbed it in the throat.

When glass shattered, I was never cut. When I got the call that there was an accident, or a death, I showed up. I had a dress to wear to the funeral. I could fit anything I needed in a carry-on bag. I remembered to bring workout shoes. I could cook in anybody's kitchen.

So often in an emergency, I was only thinking of what needed to happen, what needed to get done, that I didn't have a clue how I felt about the state of emergency, and I had even less insight if I was the subject of the crisis. I was never the one bleeding, except now I was.

I was telling a story I had told myself about survival, about shame and anger, some of it mine. Cancer interrupted that story.

When my mother was still alive, she told me I would not have to see her suffer at her death. She had already suffered her due all these years and death for her would be easy. I tried to hide how I felt her words like an open wound, but I knew she was lying.

It was easier to lie. I didn't even think about it. Lying became a reflex, a fallback deflection, muscle memory.

"I'm not worried."

"I'm just putting my head down until the surgery, and then I'll think about what happens next."

"I'm fine, really just fine."

I remember telling this same lie in the same tone to my mother. "I'll be fine."

the mother's regret

Happy? You want to be happy? Be happy you are alive.

I thought: let him go to Berlin. I'll stay here in Boston, with or without cancer. It would be a natural break. He could be a man someplace that had never known him in his previous gender, and I . . . what would be in it for me? I could be alone, in our home, which we owned together, among all our books and things, in a city we had moved to for his job, where after six years, I still didn't feel settled. It would be simple enough to tell people that I couldn't go. I was recuperating. I needed to stay in Boston. He had to go because he had to go, because we couldn't be together in the same place. I knew that if I didn't go to Berlin, I was smashing everything, choosing to end our marriage.

dick pics

> if you're raised with an angry man in your house,
> there will always be an angry man in your house.
> you will find him even when he is not there.
> and if one day you find that there is
> no angry man in your house—
> well, you will go find one and invite him in!
> —"Cut," Catherine Lacey

Often when I'm hearing a story about a couple who separates or breaks up, my first thought is not who cheated or what about the kids or who stays in the house, the first thing I think of is who pays?

My husband was a winner. He won everything left and right: grants, awards, fellowships, a literary agent, a book deal. I had dinner with the lovely children I worked with. We had cocktails and aperitifs and dessert wine. A sweet boy made pitchers of negronis. I lost my car that was parked right outside his apartment. I walked and walked in the street, on the sidewalk. I should have just leaned against a stone wall until morning or gone back to the boy's apartment, but I lost the apartment too. I was the loser.

Years earlier I had walked away from joint property and accumulated legal fees to sleep on friends' couches because I couldn't afford to keep paying half the mortgage on a place where I wasn't living and pay rent someplace else. It was a different relationship now and the same economic reality. It was my mother's economic reality. I fantasized about never waking up following surgery or discovering that the cancer had already spread everywhere and I didn't have long to live. Cut and done. This is the origin of grief; a terrible loneliness you feel next to the person closest to you. I missed my mother. I missed my wife.

the stasi men

All the dogs in Berlin had the same face. A wiry, bearded face
with intelligent eyes and perked ears. None of the dogs paid me
the slightest bit of attention even though I was so dog hungry,
missing our labradoodle and yellow Lab back home in Boston.
The German dogs trotted with purpose and never veered from
the path to chase a duck or leap into the water or bark to say *hi*
or *keep away*. This is what it means to be a good dog in Berlin.

I had chosen to go with my husband to Berlin, where he was
on an academic fellowship and I was there as "spouse of." My
position relegated me to the outer circle of the big-headed fellows, which was fine with me. It was part of the story of our
relationship—he was a front guy, I preferred to watch the scene
around me. We were also there to try and put our marriage back
together following his gender transition, now two years into this
new stage of our lives, our relationship. How would it be to live
someplace where nobody knew our specific relationship history
or had known us in a previous incarnation as a queer couple?
Were we still a queer couple? The hope was that in a setting
where somebody was cooking and cleaning for us, we would stop

fighting about whose turn it was to vacuum and what was for dinner and get to the big fights, such as, Were we going to stay married?

We were living in Wannsee, a southern suburb of Berlin, on the River Havel. While there, I visited the late summer garden at the Liebermann Villa, the summer residence of the painter Max Liebermann, on a tour with a cohort of fellows. A small birch allée leads to Lake Wannsee and features prominently in many of Liebermann's paintings. There is a bronze otter fountain, purple cabbages planted among the dahlias, a rose arbor. It is an artist's garden, with colors and secret rooms and crafted views. After Liebermann died in 1935, the house was confiscated by the Nazis. I wandered nearly next door to the Wannsee Conference Museum, an imposing villa, where in 1942 in a ninety-minute meeting, fifteen men decided "the final solution to the Jewish question" and then were served lunch and drank cognac.

at the table

At the obligatory group dinner every night, a dreamy Italian German waiter pulled out the chairs for all the women and poured endless glasses of wine with his hand over his heart. I felt lit up in the spotlight of his beautiful service. He was soft-spoken and had a delicious accent. He greeted me with warmth and eagerness, anticipated my needs, and spoke to me as though he were kissing my hand. He was my favorite. My husband sat with his elbows on the table, chatting up his fellow fellows about digital philosophy and Balkan politics and the fifteenth-century Ottoman empire.

"To reduce a gender transition to being in the wrong flesh bag in my experience is problematic."

"If the condemned recanted, the person was strangled before the fire was lit—a mercy execution."

"Neoliberalism is about the individual, not the group!"

My husband was the first trans person to be selected as a fellow for this program, to sit at this table. His award had been publicized, which mostly preempted the need for him to introduce himself as trans, which he had no hesitation about doing. It did happen, more than once, though, that when he described living as a "white, Midwestern girl from a small town in Indiana for fifty years," an audience member didn't recognize the signifier—the bearded, burly guy in the designer glasses—as the signified. "Who was the middle-aged woman from Indiana you were talking about?" he was asked.

the questions we carried

There were two single women among the fellows. When I wanted to get my girl on, we sneaked cigarettes and complimented each other's wardrobe selections. "I love your shoes!" "I love *your* shoes!" My husband called them my lesbian girlfriends. They were my favorites.

My husband liked to dress in streetwear and overpriced sneakers. He was peppy and happy and filled with joy. Before the transition, he never sweated. In Berlin, he'd sweat and sweat like a hairy, sweating man. He was proud of his sweat. "Look at this sweat," he said at the dinner table, happily sweating.

As conversations went on around me, I nodded agreeably

left and right, chewing and swallowing my German meaty meat meals—pink boar's meat ravioli, twice-cooked venison, mussels with fennel and blood oranges, lamb's lettuce with grape and bacon vinaigrette. If anybody asked me anything directly, I panicked into muteness.

"Your husband says you like to cook. Maybe you can take a cooking class during your time in Berlin."

"Perhaps you are interested in cheese culture?"

"What are the ruins of capitalism?"

Every table conversation felt like an interview for a job I was not going to get.

My husband's question for me was, Could I love a man, specifically, him? I had the same question for myself. I mean, you love the person, not a body, not a gender, and what did it matter after nearly twenty years together? People stay married for all kinds of reasons. My husband and I had a joint bank account. We shared an aesthetic sensibility, except for my disdain for streetwear and sneakers. We were both Italian. We weren't going to break up, were we?

what country is this?

"What is the point of these mandatory group dinners?" asked a slim Russian American journalist, a visiting scholar who ate nothing but the weak and weak-minded at the table.

"To enjoy each other's company?" I said, my mouth full of the most delicious plum torte, made with the tiny blue-green plums that were in season right that minute.

In a conversation about the varieties of gender, the Russian journalist said they had always felt like a boy but had learned how to be a girl. They had had a double mastectomy in 2005 and then breast reconstruction and were now taking testosterone. They described their relationship to their new body as the way one would think of inhabiting a new country. I wondered about the experience of being in relationship to a new body in a new country—like an American lesbian married to a man in Berlin.

our personal american disaster

My husband started testosterone shortly after the 2016 American presidential election, and I couldn't seem to separate the political disaster of our country from our ongoing personal disaster. I couldn't bear to listen to the news. I couldn't stop listening to the news. I had never felt so implicated by the news, by what white men in America were doing. As a queer woman in America, I thought I had sorted out my personal and political affiliations with gender years before. I mostly didn't pay attention to men unless I loved them, like my father and my nephews and a few dear friends, or they were interrupting me or talking over me or hitting on me or threatening me or taking up too much space or in my way. They didn't get my time or energy or attention. Now men were impossible to ignore. Day after day, I would open my computer, resolved to delete my social media accounts, but never delete them. Day after day, I would read my husband's latest Facebook post about navigating the men's bathroom, about drinking bourbon at a bar with other men drinking bourbon, about being called sir and boss, buddy and bro.

For twenty years, I never had to think about my identity in

relation to my marriage. I was queer in a queer marriage. Everybody saw me as queer. I saw myself as queer. What did I look
like next to a man? Not myself, not queer.

I needed to speak about his transition, but I wasn't able to—
not to our friends, my friends, my family. In spite of my husband's talking and talking about his transition, I didn't have
language or vocabulary to respond, to say my own things. He
was becoming the person he always wanted to be, the person he
always was. But in some way, I thought his transition erased our
history, my history, and invented a new present for me. "What
do you think of my beard?" my husband would ask me. I had
nothing to say. He was so happy. I put my hand over his mouth.
"Stop talking. Just shut up. Shut the fuck up."

men with pockets

One of the fellows was a Hungarian filmmaker, most of whose
films had been banned in his native country. Every day, he
wore a version of the same khaki jacket with multiple pockets.
He packed the pockets with pens and notebooks and Kleenexes
and called it his office. He was my favorite. Several of his films
were available with English subtitles, and on Monday nights we
adjourned to the library after dinner to watch his movies, often
with chocolate and brandy as though we were in a Merchant
Ivory movie. One of his films was a documentary about a con-
test sponsored by the Hungarian Young Communist League to
hire a pop band to entertain the young workers at an oil refin-
ery. In the film, the Young Communist League discusses their
criteria for the band—no hippy-length hair, no ragged jeans, no
cursing on stage, no groupies. They talk and smoke and talk and

talk—about the role of music in a political movement, about how to recruit more young people to the Young Communist League, about the seditious dangers of unbridled rock music. None of the bands audition for the job by actually playing instruments or singing together, and nothing the committee says in their talking has anything to do with music or art. Ultimately, they hire the band most compliant with their interests, which is to say social-ist Hungary's interests. The film is sad and funny, a curiously gentle illustration of the importance and impossibility of making art in a totalitarian society. With his work, the filmmaker could communicate the things he was not allowed to say.

Every morning, I would sneak down to the breakfast table before the crowd descended and fill a plate with seeded bread, a selec-tion of meats and cheeses, and fresh fruit, and I would wait for a custom-made cup of coffee. Most days, I avoided the pastries and the people. Then I would go back to our apartment and read, my little breakfast picnic spread around me. I read *Stasiland* by Anna Funder, an account published in 2003 about the condi-tions in East Berlin before the wall came down. Two hundred and seventy-four thousand people worked for the Stasi between 1950 and 1989. In a country of sixteen million people, the Stasi kept files on six million citizens. Most of these files are now in an official archive, where they are accessible to the public. They include 39 million file cards, 1.4 million photographs, 34,000 film and sound documents. Laid out end to end, these records would cover 100 kilometers—a third of the length of the Berlin Wall. The Stasi reported on everything: what time you left your apartment, where you stopped for coffee, who you talked to on the phone, who came to your home.

They kept scent samples on persons of interest, the theory being that a person's scent was as identifiable as fingerprints. Scent samples were collected by stealing an article of clothing from a suspect or by wiping a chair the suspect had sat on with a cloth that was then stored in a glass jar. Dogs were used to track suspects based on their smells. How did East Germans live like that for more than thirty years? Family members spying on each other—husbands spying on wives, children reporting on parents. When the wall came down, did they forgive one another? How did they make sense of their history? The East German peace activist and politician Vera Wollenberger discovered that her husband, the father of their two children, had spied on her throughout their marriage. She divorced him in 1992, and a decade later he wrote to her and begged for her forgiveness.

another berlin story

Since I was in Berlin, I decided to watch all of Werner Herzog's movies. And as no Herzog scholars had revealed themselves at the dinner table, I thought I might work myself up to saying something like, "That guy who got eaten by the bear, *that* was crazy, right? And what was up with his hair?" In a scene in *Fitzcarraldo* that says everything about the sanctity and stupidity of the dreams of white men, Klaus Kinski, a white Messiah in a white suit with a halo of radiant blonde hair, directs all the brown people in the jungle to haul a 320-ton steamship over a mountain.

All the young men in Germany had the same haircut: a taper fade, long on top, shaved on the sides and back. My husband is not young, but this is how his hair is cut. One day I met him at a barber shop in Schöneberg. I got there early and saw him with

shaving cream on his face getting his beard trimmed, the barber's chair tilted like a steamship heading up a mountain. His
eyes were closed in a dreamy dream of manhood and all that was
needed to complete the picture was a cigar and Caruso singing in
the background.

History is infrastructure. There is personal history, and there
is the history of a relationship. There is the history of where we
are from, the places we have lived, where we have traveled, the
dogs we have owned. I married a woman. That is my history.

the opposite of a good man

Erich Mielke was the Minister of State Security from 1957 until
the Berlin Wall fell in 1991. At the Stasi museum, I saw Mielke's
office, his private bathroom, his emergency sleeping quarters for
when he had to work late. There were pictures of him everywhere in the museum: a short, squat man with small eyes, wearing a uniform and saluting, medals spread all over his chest. He
would be less than a mouthful for the Russian journalist. They
could eat him in one bite of their Klaus Kinski mouth. But he
fancied himself a big politician, a policeman, a manly man, a
numbers man on the hunting field: a hundred dead deer gutted
and laid out on the killing field in front of him, including frozen
carcasses purchased to inflate the kill numbers.

a book club in berlin

I went to a book club of American, Canadian, and British expats
who had been living in Berlin from between ten and forty years.
Some of the book club members were married to German citi-

zens, had German family, or had connections to German history. We were reading *Stasiland*. The first comment among the readers was that the title *Stasiland* was problematic. Book club members told me they were reluctant to read the book in public. A young woman in the group said she only read it on the S-Bahn if nobody was sitting across from her on the train to see the title. "The Germans think everybody should be over this by now."

I had thought that in the book club we'd meet each other speaking a common language with shared assumptions. Not so. What I heard from the book club was that those citizen informers the Stasi employed were doing the best they could. They were working to take care of their families, to pay rent and buy food. And there was free healthcare, free education. No, it wasn't a perfect system, but better a neighbor or relative informing on you, the assumption being that maybe the informer you know wouldn't say anything too awful about you. It was a corrupt system, the book club members said, and "we were all its victims."

I wanted to draw clear lines between the good men and the bad, but they refused. Is it possible to be a good man in a corrupt system? Does the system reveal the good men or protect the bad ones?

"When I was with the opera, we did a concert at Moabit Prison in Berlin," the retired singer in the book club said. "He was there, Meilke, the few years he was locked up. He was an old man then, weak."

what can we do?

I was an American in Berlin in 2018. The daily onslaught of news from the US was unbearable. The Eastern Europeans had a shrug-and-sigh attitude about the creep or lunge toward totalitarianism. They'd been down this road, around this corner, before. When the news reported on Hungary's intensifying policy to keep the country "Christian" and reject multiculturalism and immigration, the Hungarian filmmaker whose work was banned, whose university mentor informed on him to the state, who left his home with his family to make a better life for his children in the West, said over a massive pork hock with red cabbage and a mound of spätzle, "What can you do? Make your art."

What could I do? I went to the opera. I listened to music at the Berlin Philharmonie. In a country where I didn't have language, neither the local language nor a vocabulary to express how I was feeling, I wanted to be submerged in big emotion and big sound. I wanted to be reset. I was trying to regroup. I was trying to make sense of my history and to consider an opening for my husband's new physicality, his widening shoulders and deep voice, his new name.

We saw Achim Freyer's production of Verdi's *Requiem* at the Deutsche Oper. The production was a fantastic moving frieze of repeating characters in black and white and red. The procession was relentless and mechanical. The staging suggested a language of object and color about mourning. Was I in mourning for my queer marriage?

In November in Berlin, when everyone else was wearing black or gray, my husband wore bright yellow sweatpants and a blue short-sleeved T-shirt with the sleeves rolled up so you could see all his tattoos. When we walked along the East Side Gallery with all the murals painted on the remnant of the Berlin Wall, he looked like part of the artwork.

At the Collectors Room Berlin there was an exhibit called *The Wunderkammer Olbricht,* a personal collector's exhibit with objects from the Renaissance and Baroque periods. It was like a writing prompt curiosity cabinet full of little odd things with stories to tell—a ten-foot-long narwhal tooth that visitors could touch and make a wish upon; a miniature, anatomically correct replica of a pregnant woman carved out of ivory; iridescent-green scarab beetles as big as a man's hand. My husband and I visited the exhibit, and we each picked out an object as our personal talisman. My husband chose a small gold and enamel turning head from about 1600 that likely hung on the end of a ten-bead rosary. One face is a skull and the other is a beautiful youth. My pick was an object *naturalia,* a porcupine pufferfish, fierce and menacing.

The man who is still my husband and I walked around the lake at Schlachtensee. He was wearing sneakers that looked like a three-ring circus on his feet. His sneakers could have led a parade. He'd never seemed more easy with himself, unconfined in a body that felt like his. He was my favorite. All the people on the path couldn't help looking at his footwear in their restrained German way. The German dogs looked at us both with love. This is what makes them the good dogs.

the ghosts in our marriage

Living is a constant recitation of partial losses, ebbing daily up to the shore of our being: every act of speech and love and longing reintroduces a rend, a gap, a tear.
—*Called Back,* Mary Cappello

I was seeing a helping professional in Boston nearly every week. She was so young she was still on her first marriage, but then everybody was so much younger than I was then. She said we were working on the progression of identity and I had to introduce myself to people, say words out loud. You would think by the age of sixty my identity would be formed and I'd already have met all the people I'm going to know. I had nothing to say. "You never tell us anything," my friends complained. "Everything changed," they say, "but you stayed the same. How are you?" I said, "No good ever came from talking about anything."

We were all in the bathroom in our condo in the Jamaica Plain neighborhood of Boston—three men and me. I wanted to get out of the bathroom. My husband was talking to the two worker guys: *This is fucked up* and *This is not fucking acceptable* and *The schedule is fucked* and *Fuck this fucking shit, I mean look at this fucking shit, I'm not paying for this fucked up fucking shit.*

I wanted to get out of the bathroom, get away from all the *fucks,* but there were too many men in there and they were all standing in the doorway. I thought the guys and my husband were having a fight. They were all yelling *fuck* at each other and then they were laughing and still saying *fuck fuck yeah right* and *yeah*. I was saying nothing.

"You blocked me in the bathroom," I said later. "I couldn't get out and please don't talk like that when I'm standing right there. I don't like it. I don't want the worker guys talking like that in front of me, and if you do it, it gives them permission to join in."

Talk like what? That's how guys talk.

I was right there.

What difference does that make?

I was right there. I was trapped in the bathroom. Do you talk like that in front of your students?

What are you talking about? Look, I was just trying to get those guys in line. It's been three months. We need a fully functioning bathroom.

And I am saying don't talk like that in front of me when there are other people around, especially other guys. It's about respect.

Respect? This is about managing a project.

That was the first time I can remember hating my husband, although not the first time I have hated a man.

In 2016, when my husband started transitioning, he said he was the same person, only now he had a body that more closely aligned with how he had always seen himself. With such a body he could be more present, more himself, happy. But I didn't recognize who he had become. He went from being a small, slight queer woman to a stocky, bearded guy. Maybe more to the point, or maybe just to my point, I didn't recognize myself in this new partnership configuration. He thought becoming a man was a small shift in our marriage, a discarding of parts and pronouns and costumes so that I would see what he had been feeling all along.

During the transition, I started forgetting things. Maybe not *started*. I had always forgotten a lot of things: I've forgotten if it snowed on my February birthday last year. What were your birthday traditions, a friend asked? I tried to remember: Breakfast out, a gift from my mother beautifully wrapped, cradled in tissue paper, a robe or a purse that would likely be returned. The gifts from lovers—leather pants, a suede jacket with fringe, silver earrings, German chocolate cake. As a bullheaded young feminist, I ranted against material conventions of domesticity—crystal and china patterns, window treatments, 600-thread count sheet sets. I didn't want to be tied down to things. I wanted agile living, unencumbered: two forks, two plates, one pan. On my thirtieth birthday, my mother bought me a set of dishes that I never would have picked out for myself, but I used them for decades. I know they were an acknowledgment of sorts that I set my own table in my own kitchen. She worried how I would put a household together, two girls together, no hope chest, no wedding registry. During the transition, for my birthday, my husband bought me four blue dishes, so big, so heavy, I recognized nothing of my own taste in them. Whose table were these meant for I wondered? Was I to be the wife at this table setting?

I've forgotten keyboard shortcuts, how to prevent salt from clumping, measurement conversions. Every time I made meatballs, I called my mother. "Do I cook the chopped onions before adding them to the hamburger mixture, or can I add them raw? Fresh parsley or dried?" I've forgotten my nieces' birthdays, my wedding anniversary. I didn't marry *him* anyway, I married *her*. I have never been able to keep dates and numbers in my leaky mind. Which concerns me, because I'm a writer; I rely on knowing who I am based on who and where I've been. I've lost track of pronouns, of who I am in relation to the people around me. I call him my partner, significant other, spouse. When I talk to people, I don't call him *my husband*. I talked to my mother every morning in the years before her death. "What was the name of that song?" she asked me. "About the dream that's over?" I yelled at the bathroom contractor that I had no idea workers were coming one morning, and he showed me a text he had sent the day before saying they would be at the house by eight. I said *fuck* but not out loud.

The things my husband needed in the house at all times were half-and-half and ginger ale. *Did you pick up half-and-half for tomorrow's coffee? Do we have ginger ale?* I forgot. Again. Maybe I was at war in my mind with his priorities. He didn't want a ginger ale right that minute, but he wanted ginger ale available at all times—ginger ale as a necessity for living. I was surprised over and over when I opened the linen closet or looked under the sink and we were out of toilet paper, dishwasher soap, laundry detergent. I forgot what we needed to live. If my husband were to ask me what I needed, what would say? I had no idea what my own life necessities were. Maybe if we were still two women together, I would remember: windows facing east, a horizon line, a slotted spoon.

My mother was not a happy woman. She most often blamed my

father for her unhappiness, or her children, whose welfare she thought she was protecting by staying with her husband. As a kid, in case the fighting became apocalyptic and I had to leave in a hurry, I kept a getaway bag packed with a flashlight, wooden matches, a pocketknife, Band-Aids, a length of rope, and fishhooks. What book would I pack? Maybe *The Swiss Family Robinson,* so I would know how to leach the poison from cassava and build an aqueduct. My mother left once and stayed overnight at a Quality Inn a few miles from the house, but she was scared to be alone and came home the next day.

Along with forgetting things during the transition, I was dropping things: coffee cups, plates, dog bowls, books, car keys. My hands couldn't be trusted. I dropped the salt box in the soup, the top to the cayenne pepper jar in the salad dressing. I dropped my husband's blue coffee cup that he bought in London in October 2017 when I was not traveling with him in the sink. The cup cracked. We both thought the crack was prophetic, that our marriage was broken. I slept with my hands curled into fists under my pillow. The leaves of the azalea looked scorched. I had to keep cutting to reach clean, healthy wood. One minute I was trimming the suckers and dead branches, and the next the pruners escaped from my hands and landed in the mulch and rotting leaves.

I worried that I had dementia, MS, a brain tumor, a neurological disorder affecting my coordination and brain function. I recorded myself talking, reading. Was I slurring my words? Was I losing track of my thoughts? Why. Was. I. Speaking. So. Slowly. While my thoughts were racing racing.

I know how grief can translate into physical symptoms. A few weeks after my mother died and the busyness of death subsided, my father thought he was dying too. He sat in a dark room, went to the doctor, but he was fine. On the phone every morning he told me what he fixed for breakfast, what pills he took. He wanted a witness. He worried about food in the refrigerator, in the pantry, still there since her death. There was a lemon, some cheese, her homemade salad dressing in the green shaker jar. I got rid of the fruit, the cold cuts. "Throw it out, Dad," I told him. He couldn't do it. He asked me what to do with the frozen peaches, the containers of sauce she had made and stored in the freezer. He was haunted by food she wasn't there to cook. "Sometimes I wake up at night," he said, "and I have a pain."

When my father died, it was not unexpected. He was ill. He made up his mind not to drag out his death—everybody had to get back to work—and then he was dead. The morning of his funeral, my youngest brother came to the funeral home and said he would meet us at the church. He needed to see his doctor for an EKG, maybe a stress test. He had a pain.

Men feel pain as a pressure in the chest. They don't know that is what it feels like to be sad.

My husband said that he was worried about my mind. He worried about my mind when something happened and we disagreed about what it was, when I heard him say something that he said later he never said, when he heard a tone from me that

I didn't intend. Every conversation between us left us stunned and reeling.

I didn't say that.

That's what I heard.

But that's not what I said.

You said . . .

Why are you yelling?

I'm not yelling.

What would your husband think, asked the guy with the Brezhnev eyebrows sitting next to me on the plane—he was a musician with one of the Boston orchestras and had invited me to a rehearsal of an upcoming concert—*if we had dinner together?* I was telling him about the Piano Salon Christophori in the Berlin neighborhood of Wedding where the very reasonable price of your ticket gets you a free drink and world class musicians in an old factory. My husband? I had my well-used comeback at the ready: I'm married to a woman. But I wasn't anymore. Did being a woman married to a man now somehow flip a switch and reengage the attention of men, attention I had ducked for years?

I threw away the bath towels and bought new ones because I thought the towels smelled like him, a peppery, shoe leather, locker room smell. Has his smell changed? a girlfriend asked me. Is smell linked to gender? That would be a deal breaker for me, she said.

I was driving from Jamaica Plain to Cambridge where all the

helping professionals work, which depending on the time of day, can be zippy or can take a lifetime of regrets. It was July, the roads were clear, the sky overcast. There was no sun in my eyes. I used GPS anywhere I drove in Boston, but lately I was missing prompts, missing the tricky lane changes to turn onto the Boston University Bridge over the Charles River—a route I've driven a thousand times. I made a left onto Highland and drifted toward the right lane. Somebody was honking. I jerked the steering wheel to the left, more honking. There was danger all around. A guy in a white van pulled up next to me. I didn't want to hear what he had to say. I kept going and turned into a parking lot on Chester a short distance away. The van pulled up behind me and blocked me in. *Now and at the hour of our death.* I decided I should record my death so my loved ones would know what happened. I fumbled with my phone, but I couldn't remember my passcode. My phone didn't recognize me.

Hey, the guy in the truck said, *are you okay? Oh hey, don't be scared. I'm not mad, but I had the right of way. You were all over the road, and you clipped me and I just wanted to make sure you're okay. Did you even see me? My truck is fine, but there's paint transfer on your car.*

He touched my car, a blessing for my safe passage.

I thought I was having a heart attack. A tightness in my throat, pressure in my chest. I couldn't speak, my ears felt plugged. This happened when I was driving and the news came on—all the angry men yelling—or when I was in my car a block from home and I thought of something I forgot to pick up, a prescription or dry cleaning, ginger ale again. Everything felt weighted with too much meaning and significance. Better not to do anything. I couldn't fall asleep at night unless I was listening to a book or a podcast. At a writing residency, I met a young woman, anxious in the way all young people are anxious these days. Who will love her? What will she be? How will she ever pay off her student loans? She listened to the same gay comedic writer every night to fall asleep, which she had been doing for the past four years. Every night? I asked. What about when you have a real boyfriend in your bed? My real boyfriend is the writer, she said. I nodded. Night after night I listened to the same book, a story of a reckoning of a life and a consideration of faith. The narrator's voice was reassuring, measured: "I'll pray, and then I'll sleep." The listening was a kind of prayer for me, and yet I could become unconscious in a moment anytime during the day. The dogs and I piled on the bed in the afternoon and slept and slept until we all wanted dinner. Wake up! Wake up! Who will feed us? Me, again.

Are you getting dressed in the morning? Leaving the house? the doctor asked me. Are you spending time with people, talking to your friends? Are you experiencing tunnel vision? Vertigo? Lightheadedness? How many alcoholic beverages do you consume in a week? Do you feel safe in your home? In this America? When a partner transitions, she said, the whole family transitions.

My mind was very busy, very buzzy, but if I tried to track the thoughts that kept piling up in heaps and mounds, they all led to "What can I eat now?"

I was meeting a friend for coffee just one T stop away. I thought I would walk, but I got turned around, lost my way. I was late and rushing and sweating and my friend texted that he couldn't wait. He left. I left too and returned home. I was afraid to sit by myself at the coffee shop. Was this how I would become my mother?

All my dreams were about driving or reading. I couldn't see the road, there was a blizzard, ice covered the windshield and I couldn't see through it. I couldn't make out the words on the page, the road signs. The words were blurred, shifting, microscopic. Since the 2016 election, all the news was the same recurring nightmare. I drove right off the road into wordless silence.

My husband said, *You need a structure, a routine—you could go through those boxes in the basement, organize the pantry. I'd like it if you made that chicken again.* My wife had never spoken to me like that. Was that true? Was this the husband in my dreams talking or my real husband?

I never wanted to be anyone's wife, I thought.

If I got new glasses the way would become clear, I thought.

I prepared to make my escape. I kept my phone charged. I expected a news alert: Get out now.

Some couples keep their money separate. He joins a private golf course. She changes the china with the dining room wall color. I know couples who don't watch the same movies, who vote differently. These were not our problems. Some husbands gamble, watch all the sports, collect guns. Some husbands open the refrigerator and say over their shoulder, "Do we have any eggs?"

Pick up the jar of mayo and say, "What is the expiration date on this?"

Outside every closed door where my helping professional saw clients, there was a white-noise machine that masked conversations between helping professionals and clients. In the waiting room, I felt cocooned in the sound of a million whispers. Inside my helping professional's light-filled office, I often heard sounds from the street outside: emergency vehicle sirens, car doors slamming, breaking glass. Danger was everywhere. I thought I needed a white-noise machine to carry with me. My helping professional had the glow of exhaustion of a saint or a new mother. I would have liked to feed her a bowl of soup, a piece of bread. I would have liked to curl up on her couch and nap in the white noise of her voice.

My history felt crowded, heaped with bowls of cereal, so many books, cities, songs, loved ones. If I put aside all the memories that started with "grandmother" and "mother," like moving boxes out of the basement, would that make room for new memories? Would there be new boxes filled with who I am, who he is now?

For my husband's fiftieth birthday, before he started testosterone, before pronoun debates, there was a party in Minneapolis, followed by a hiking trip in Utah. My husband didn't want to turn fifty, didn't want a party, didn't want to play his old self with our old friends. I planned the party because I wanted the familiarity of a place where we had been happy—where I thought we were happy anyway—and to be around people who loved us. In Utah, amid the red and orange landscape, he told me he was planning on killing himself when he turned fifty. He didn't want to live another year as a woman, even as a woman I loved. Was that woman the ghost in our marriage?

I read about a woman with the ability to recall details of events that happened on specific days over decades of her life. Not just what she did on her twenty-seventh birthday, but what the weather was like on the day she moved to LA, the day when she was nine and came home sick from school and her mom made her chicken noodle soup. But she can't sort and discard "good" memories from "bad," so all the memories play on a loop in her head: the argument with her college roommate, the closing of that karaoke bar, her husband's death fifteen years ago, over and over, and the emotional effect is as if she is experiencing the event in present tense. "I'm always looking back, whether I want to or not, and sometimes I am there whether or not I want to be."

For two years I replayed the memories of our relationship over and over: on this day last year we were walking on a rocky coastline in Maine, two years ago we met our new nephew, my hair was longer then, your father was still sitting in the blue recliner watching Notre Dame football, I grew delicata squash that summer, you hadn't become a swimmer yet.

"Do you ever see P——?" my husband's mother asked me. She has Alzheimer's and remembered we had married but didn't remember that her daughter had transitioned. We Facetimed with her nearly every night. She called us her girls. We didn't correct her. We took turns visiting her, so when I traveled to see her in the care facility in St. Paul, my husband was usually not with me. "I like blueberries on my cereal," she said. I watched her running water over some blueberries. She turned off the water. Turned on the water. "Did you want these?" she asked me. She doesn't remember *blueberries*. "Do you still love her?"

Where should I put the memories of our history before the transition? More boxes in the basement? The crossword puzzles, the million games of phone Boggle, all the seasons of college basketball. Wait, those are *his* memories, not mine, and are not part of his life present tense. Are shifting interests gendered? Does he still hate Duke? Will he remember that the crossword answer *ere* means an old English word for *before*. I am remembering a version of him that no longer existed.

The artist Louise Bourgeois could invent other realities with her hands. She said, "Some of us are so obsessed with the past that we die of it. . . . Every day you must accept the past and abandon it, and if you can't accept it, then you have to do sculpture." Testosterone reshaped the planes and angles of my husband's head. I'd like to sculpt his head out of metal and glass, add eight legs. I touched him through his clothes that all looked like gym clothes. He was flexed and braced, as though a storm was coming. We were in a storm. Or I could build a cage, a cell, and put inside photos of our wedding, the hiking trip to Ireland, all the dogs, and then lock the door. No Trespassing.

My husband made new friends with young bearded men, with car service drivers and valets, with salespeople, service providers, the young gay guys who flirt with him, the bartenders. I called them all my grandsons.

We were meeting some friends for brunch in Providence. My girl-friends. It was a beautiful fall day in a city that has just enough history and ruin to make me love it. We strolled over cobble-stone streets to the restaurant, sidewalks buckled from push-ing tree roots. Mary directed our attention to the name and date plaques on houses more than 150 years old, the hand-painted tile house numbers, and the wedding cake house, which was once the residence and dressmaking enterprise of the Tirocchi sisters. We sat together at a table near a window facing the street where families, couples, dogs walked and walked. I was sitting across the table from my husband. He was checking his phone. From time to time, he looked out the window with avid interest and longing. All at once I realized I was at brunch with the girls, and he was not. He was a man sitting at the table wondering how long before he could get up and go.

In the dining room in our condo in Jamaica Plain hung a paint-ing by a Mexican artist called *El fantasma en sus vidas*. There are four figures in the frame and two indefinite shadow figures. One is just an outline, the other looks like a previous version, a pentimento of one of the fully formed figures. One of them could have been me. I was a ghost in my own life. Or maybe she was a ghost in mine.

After the death of the jumping licking panting black dog, who had been the yellow Lab's lifelong companion, the Lab seemed not himself. Perhaps he was in mourning. This was our first year in Boston, before my husband's transition. The Lab stood facing a corner and did not turn his head when I called him. He moped and sighed, restless and anxious. He didn't want to run or play and only perked up when a black dog was in his vicinity. We practiced new tricks for something to do together. Twirl, weave, head down. Listening to Joni Mitchell under a yellow afghan seemed to soothe him. Our first spring in our condo in Jamaica Plain, we thought a new puppy would bring him around, but it seemed to rush him to the end. Although we loved her madly, the new puppy did not bring me and my husband around either. We all seemed to be rushing to the end.

My husband was leaning back on the couch talking on the phone. He was talking about sneakers and beard trimmers and bourbon. I looked at him. He looked like a boxer, a little thick, broad across his chest and back from swimming laps, solid. I didn't recognize the sound of his laugh. He rubbed his head, stretched the skin under his chin. I was surprised that he didn't have an Adam's apple. And then I remembered. I was becoming less surprised by who he was.

Night after night and nearly every morning, we heard the nine-year-old son of our neighbor next door yell, "You do it! I'm not doing it! Fucking unfair! Fucking unfair fuck!" The fall we were in Berlin, the child's fifty-year-old mother, the same age as my husband at the time, dropped dead in her bedroom on a Sunday morning. Sometimes the yelling was a duet between father and son: "I'm not your fucking maid! Pick up your jacket. Every day it's the same bullshit." Karen had sung Motown in her kitchen on Sunday mornings, called her boy "Rabbit," and was the communication conduit between our two-household condo. In the summer I'd meet her Fridays after work on our bluestone patio for a glass of wine and a recap of a television series we were both watching, except if there was a school shooting. Then she stayed inside. She played basketball with the boy in the driveway at the height-adjustable hoop and walked to Dunkin holding his hand. One time taking the dogs out, I saw her husband sitting in his car smoking a cigar in front of the house. When I got back with the dogs, he was still there. I texted Karen, Is everything okay? She was not surprised that her husband was hiding in his car. She texted back, Yes, just too much family time. There had been no evidence of the bad heart that killed her. Her husband and son are stunned and stricken without her. Unloading groceries from his car, the husband kicked the car door closed, then kicked it again, told me being a single mother was the worst. He looked like he needed a haircut, maybe vitamins. I could hear the aftermath of loss every day. What will the boy put in the new boxes in his basement? Karen and I and all the ghost wives and mothers were drinking wine while the ghost dogs and daughters played in the yard. Over the next year, the yelling rose and fell, sometimes the wails of heartbreak, ascending into rage at the injustices of life.

men i love

brian, the guest at the party, 1981

I was at a party. It was Minneapolis in June, the most perfect time of year to be at a Minnesota backyard barbeque porch party with neighbors and friends and friendly strangers. The lesbian scuba divers passed around photos from their latest dive, while a gay gardener in overalls strummed a ukelele and a woman with forearms like a pro wrestler pumped the shiny silver keg. The food table was loaded with midwestern salads—lots of mayo and ranch dressing and boiled potatoes—served with charred hot-dogs and chips fast wilting in the heat. I drank beer from a bottle, wearing sunglasses and a sleeveless shell to expose my tanned and Nautilus-toned arms. It was summer, which meant light—lightweight linen and empty pockets, heavy hair lifted up and off my neck, as well as late nights, loose-fitting clothes, and living lightly, in a constant state of readiness for everything. I had a girlfriend—who didn't come to the party—a full tank of gas. A young guy in shorts and a T-shirt with a little squish around his middle, a long dark ponytail, and an open round face sat on the back porch steps. I looked at him and thought, Do I know him? I couldn't place him, but I felt strongly that we had met. I thought,

I *know* him, like a childhood friend who knew me when I was young and unformed, whose family my family knew from the neighborhood, where we nodded at each other in the vestibule of the church our families went to, which had to have happened in a different city from the city where we were now.

He noticed me looking and smiled in my direction. He wasn't "my type," if a gay girl could have a type of guy she was—I was—attracted to. When I dated men, I liked swarthy and brooding guys, hard-bodied with lush, curly hair, or guys who were pretty, smooth as a porn star. But there was something. I walked over and sat down on the porch step below him. Without any preliminaries, I picked up his hand. We were holding hands. This could be my alternative, unimagined life with a man who made lentil soup and shivered when I touched his wrist. I thought about eating toast with him, crumbs in his beard, walking hand in hand through the farmer's market. So easy. Easier than being a big homo? Easier than being with a woman? A man who looked at me with uncomplicated love and said, "I would dig a garden for you." There were calluses on his palm. If I had grown up with a boy from the neighborhood who, when I climbed too high in a tree and was afraid to come down, drove his father's car under the tree so I could step on the roof and sit down, sliding to the ground, could he be this boy? Could I fall into, fall down, and land safely in the kingdom of heterosexuality?

We weren't looking at each other and then we were. "Do you want to stay or should we leave now?" he said. Where were we going? I couldn't think about what was happening. He put his arm around my shoulders, leaned his head toward mine. There was nothing aggressive or pushy about his gestures, more *Here we are again.* Before we got up to leave together, I thought, *I've missed you so much.*

corey, the dog walker, 2020

He was so young. There was an infinite sweetness about him, the sweetness of an angel or a drug addict. He opened doors; drove with certainty and confidence on Boston's cow path origin roadways, changing lanes without hesitation, one hand on the wheel; passed plates at the table without being asked; kissed me on the cheek every time he said hello or good-bye like the perfect Italian grandson; he was the boyfriend you'd invite to move in after the first date. I loved how he loved our bad dogs, even when our blonde Lab rescue dog was humping the pillows on the couch and spinning on leash. He was a man who was a boy, which made him a perfect guide through boyhood for my newly trans husband. They went to the gym and the barber together, shopped for sneakers, gave each other matching leather bracelets. A man who gave me hope that it might be possible for me to love a man. I stopped holding my breath when he was around, stopped anticipating the next bad thing: that my husband would get in a fight with a passenger on the T who bumped into him in a way my husband interpreted as aggressive, or that the blond Lab would pull a whole pizza off the counter and eat it box and all. When I got weepy on mezcal margaritas—lamenting that I was losing my lesbian marriage through my husband's transition, that the dogs would never stop barking—he escorted me over curbs and down sidewalks until I found a sobering wall I could lean against. Loving him was reassuring and settling, a little medicating, a safety net over our family that seemed to be in danger of falling apart. I worried about his spending, his disregard of time and schedules, his inability to feed himself except with trash food and vending machine snacks; he repeatedly lost his keys and wallet, slapping his pockets front to back like a dance move. How is it possible to be a good man in this world? "I thought we were stronger," said my husband. We should never overestimate a person's strength just because it is convenient to do so. In the lockdown, we all lost track, lost connection, lost a righteous belief in a "positive outcome"; the dog walker slept in his car, the dogs went unwalked, we howled and howled. I lost a deep faith that love superseded bodies and body parts, pronouns and shared history. The dog walker lost his sobriety. Crossing the street—living—became a high-wire act, weaving in and out around cars, bodies, and viruses—where was the wall to lean against, the hand on my arm, the easy exhalation, that beautiful boy at my table, my wife in my bed. Wash your hands, wash your hands. We infect and are infected by one another.

the father, always

I remember my father crying maybe three times in my life. The first time was from physical pain. He slipped on ice in our driveway in the North County of St. Louis and fell on his elbow, shattering it. It was early morning. He was leaving for work and driving us to the bus stop, or maybe to school? He raised the garage door, or he stepped off the porch, and he slipped. He was wearing a shirt and tie, slick-soled shoes, carrying lunch in a paper bag my mother had packed: two sandwiches, an apple, something home-baked. Both his parents had died when he was a young man. He rarely overate, never sweated through his shirt even when he was mowing the lawn in the St. Louis summer heat and humidity. He quit smoking in the seventies, drank a glass of red wine every day after dinner. He sipped, never gulped. Year after year, he always looked exactly the same. That's what Aunt

Jennie said. Even when we first got out of the car after driving for fifteen hours from St. Louis to Buffalo, he was not wrinkled or worn. Aunt Jennie called him Mr. Clean. "Frank, you look good, you look good." For years and years his hair never thinned or grayed. He never lost or gained weight. He was a man of moderation and self-control except when it came to his family. Then he had no limits, no restrictions. He emptied his pockets, washed an endless line of cars in the driveway, tracked gas mileage for oil changes, waited up, dozing on the couch, until everybody was safely home. He was a man who tried to embody the perfect man, if the perfect man was resistant to deep feeling, financial insecurity, and pain. He was our family fixture, not impervious, not skilled at renovating or repair, but he painted walls, climbed ladders, scored a cross into chestnuts before roasting. When he cried, cradling his broken arm, my mother said, "Stop it, Frank, you're scaring the kids," a proclamation so without mercy that it made me more afraid of my mother than of my father in pain.

His past is sometimes more real to me than my own present. I live more conscious of the dead and their lives. Sometimes we confused our relationship to each other. He introduced me as his wife, his mother. Did he forget I was his daughter? Growing up, we were a secret club. We'd meet to talk about my mother. What was our responsibility to her happiness?

The second time I remember my father crying was when my Uncle Joseph Arcara died. Joe was the husband of my mother's older sister, a firefighter, who died of a massive heart attack at only fifty-one. Our family traveled from St. Louis to Buffalo to attend the funeral. I was ten. My father was in his early forties. I had seen adults cry before—my mother in particular, who cried

often about missing Buffalo, and so many people cried when
John F. Kennedy was assassinated, but this was the first time I
remember seeing people I knew, my aunts and uncles and cousins—my father included—weep with such extravagant unselfcon-
sciousness. We came together to mourn, a ritual forever marked
for me by people and food. It was July. There were platters of
thinly sliced cold cuts and cheeses, breaded veal cutlets that you
ate in a hard roll, bread and olives, roasted red peppers, sliced
melons, and green and purple grapes. The shrimp cocktail was
on ice, and there was wine and beer, with shots of Black Velvet,
the whiskey Uncle Joe drank.

At the time I thought of tears as some sort of inevitable physical expression that sneaked up on you when you read about
a dog dying or any page of *Black Beauty,* when other forms of
expression—flying, vanishing, mind control—are denied to you.

I had thought of myself, when I thought of myself at all as
more than hungry, or tired, or nervous, as a center of my family's universe. When our family visited Buffalo, I was kissed
and hugged, fed and overfed, until my face was exhausted from
smooching and chewing and swallowing. At every visit I was
scrutinized and assessed, frequently photographed, a beloved
first-born child, uncomfortable in the spotlight of so much attention and expectation. I didn't know myself yet, and where I went
to meet myself was story. I didn't know that grownups could be
sad, that their grief could outweigh their notice of me, that people I relied on for comfort and support could turn away, hide
their faces in their hands and wail. When I saw my father cry
in simple grief in the company of so many family members who
were beloved to me, who made up some core essence of myself,
I felt unloosed from the earth, that the world had tilted in some
way I didn't understand and I was at risk of disintegrating and
blowing away.

All those people are dead now—the aunts and uncles, so many cousins. I went to funerals, and I knew what to do from watching what they did at other funerals. When death comes, no matter the relationship, the love returns. Feed the mourners, hold onto the living. *Prepare to follow.*

When my father was older, he experienced the deaths of brothers and cousins, his aunt and uncle, his goombadi Tibby, his wife. I don't remember him crying, although he could have. Did he cry at my brother's wedding when the bride's parents would not join the reception dinner until all the carafes of wine had been removed from the tables, nearly fatally embarrassing my parents, who had paid for the dinner? Did he cry when I told my parents I was gay? My mother did—hot, angry tears that fell endlessly for years and years. Did he cry watching old movies alone in the near dark?

How much is possible to know about a parent's private moments, their secret sorrows? How well do we ever know the people we love? There was a story my dad and his brothers shared about a secret sister named Laura. Laura sometimes helped their mother in the house. She wasn't a sister, she was a cousin, somebody's illegitimate daughter, a neighborhood girl. We didn't know who she was, my dad said. I wanted to know. Who was she? What happened to her? Everything I feel returns to the dead somehow.

I was visiting my father after he had been diagnosed with lymphoma in January. He would be dead by March. I liked to cook for him although there were more and more things that he couldn't eat anymore. Cooking was something I could do, like cleaning or shopping. I bought him new kitchen dishcloths, new pants to accommodate his dwindling frame, another pair of slippers. For the first time he agreed to wear cardigan sweaters, which he had always dismissed as old man sweaters. There was a glass of wine in front of him. I got up to carry our plates to the sink. Windows surrounded the eating area in the kitchen. It was already dark out and the table, the glass of wine, and my father were reflected in the glass. I looked up from the counter, and he was softly crying at the table. Past, present, and future were all reflected in the glass. Pull the shades, he wept, pull the shades. You've left me to look into the dark.

the teacher of writing and life, 2010–2022

His end was that simple. Len had heard the leaking sounds of his heart clearer every day of his life. Now, those train whistles traveled away, whispering, falling quiet.
—"Ladies Room," Kevin McIlvoy

At the summer residency he wore a blue short-sleeved shirt with a straight hem, black jeans. He was tall and slim, and at the graduation dance parties he danced with his eyes closed, in an ecstatic communion with the occasion, the setting, the sweaty crowd. I was skittish around men, especially tall men, or men in authority, or men I reported to. I was not skittish around him. He was my teacher.

School had always been a mystery to me. I was making it up as I went along. I thought it was too late for grad school. I thought stories came fully formed: start at the beginning and write to the end. Just getting to work on time day after day seemed an impossible way to live. I made a chart with Post-it notes and color highlighting. I checked everything off. I got into grad school.

I thought because I was already so old, fifty-five, when I started my MFA at the Warren Wilson Program for Writers, I already knew everything. In my personal essay that accompanied my application, I said I wanted to go to grad school because at long last I saw "the value of formal training in my chosen field, the necessity of credentials, and the importance of being connected to an academic institution or a professional organization," but what I really thought was *I'm too old for this shit.* He said, "You are inviting a radical transformation in the big picture of your life as an artist."

He was my mentor, who became my friend, my touchstone, my teacher in the way that teaching is about reciprocal transformation between teacher and student. I was coming to my MFA from twenty years in advertising and publishing. I had an iron-clad corporate persona with occasional and ill-fated lapses of judgment: the hot tub with naked colleagues, the happy hours that extended overnight, the inappropriately expressed rage toward administrative inanity ("If I had a knife I would stab you all and watch your dirty red blood spill across this table"). He said, "Consider the whip tail charge—we hear the whip crack as it is cast back; we hear it crack at its coil; we hear it crack as it's cast forward."

Whether or not I had any idea what he was talking about, I entered the subject anyway. I trusted him with my clumsy words and pages thick with images and atmosphere, and for perhaps the first time in my education, I knew the great pleasure of learning.

We would often speak about loss. Death was our familiar. He had lost several friends, a community, a landscape, his health. He didn't tell me details or complete stories, he spoke as though we were continuing a conversation we had started long ago. It was the same with books I'd never read, music I hadn't heard. He invoked the names of dead friends and family, the subjects and authors of books and stories, a blues phrasing as though the dead were in conversation with us, the books sitting on the table in front of us, music in the air. These dips into the strange didn't seem strange to me at all. I was writing a series of prose pieces at the time about memory spaces—empty rooms, ruins, abandoned buildings, lost views. My teacher's seeing enlarged my own sight. There were no clear beginnings, no hard-stop endings. Everything was informed and expanded by everything. This was a storytelling that met my own aesthetic, a way of being that I aspired to. He said, "We look for the end inside the beginning; to have been, to be, to remember."

Since his death, I have looked for him everywhere. I catch a glimpse, a rare note in Little Walter's harmonica, the wail of Nina Simone, an irresistible fiddle. The world intrudes—with death, or life—with houses sold, shoes purchased, cigarettes smoked. I remember him. We once shared a common language where we met.

carl, the husband, 1998–present

Before he was my husband, he was my girlfriend, my wife, but that is only one significant point. He was nearly too anxious to leave the house, to walk the dogs, to finish his dissertation. He lived with all his things spread out on every surface to avoid the risk of losing anything, but also because there was no hierarchy of value—everything had the same worth, received the same level of interest, until it didn't, until he moved on.

Why do you keep this stuff? I asked him. Wonder Woman comic books, a collection of action figures including G.I. Jane and a bearded G.I. Joe, ceramic owls, so many keychains and rocks. How did so many different objects convey meaning? I put things together, form patterns, build equations. I want things to make some kind of sense.

I was already so old, and he was so young when we met. That's changed over twenty-five years. Sometimes he has seemed younger than he is. There was a long stretch when he reverted to a thirteen-year-old boy, smelly and loud, his hands in his pants all the time. Sometimes I have been as immature, as haphazard as an adolescent, pouting and self-absorbed: But how do you like my hat? We seem closer to the same age now, although not consistently.

In the beginning he called me A-line because that was my preferred style of dress. I wasn't ready for the next relationship, and he didn't know how to spell my name. Was it Lynette with one *n* or two? He dragged me out the kitchen sliding glass door into the dog yard, into a new life together. When my parents came to Minneapolis to meet him, I grilled the Italian sausage from Cossetta's. He talked too much and met my mother's anxiety with his own. The first time we drove to Indiana to meet his parents, to eat his own Italian mother's meatballs, I thought we could be family.

My husband is the kind of person who can orate at the spur of the moment—glass raised, a toast at the table, an impromptu speech, a strategy, explanation, an excuse. I, on the other hand, usually rehearse my words before speaking. I can't think if I'm talking, while my husband can think and talk and build worlds at the same time. I am often blank in animated discussions, especially in groups, while he is prone to saying too much and blurting. I can do a comprehensive summary of a group discussion, and in any group, he sets the tone and maneuvers the agenda. Sometimes I like to ask him questions when he is half asleep, such as "On the subject of boundaries, not as related to a therapeutic concept but visible and invisible boundaries . . ." It's not a specific question, it's more like an ignition point: *There are boundaries of past and present, of memory . . . Boundaries mark where we belong, the gateways we pass through, the thresholds we cross over . . . Migration patterns are a type of invisible boundary . . .* His mind is as deft and agile as a bird in flight, as rapid-fire and annihilating as a series of doors slamming shut one after another, as surprising as the winning argument from the television defense attorney that causes the jury to gasp.

THE FIGHTS: SPENDING AND CLEANING, TIME AND SPACE

Don't forget we have that thing next weekend.
   What thing?
   That thing I told you about.
   I'll be out of town.
   This is the first I'm hearing about it.
   I'm sure I told you.
   Why is everything we do dependent on your schedule. What about my time, my schedule?
   Your time is your time.
   It's not my time! It's only my time at your convenience, dependent on your schedule. I wouldn't have made plans if I'd known you weren't going to be here.
   I know I told you.
   I know I checked with you before making plans.
   I won't be here.

When we needed a reset, to remember who we were, we went to

an old school Italian joint in St. Paul. We held hands across the table and ate spaghetti and meatballs, fried calamari, and drank red wine in short glasses. If we were early enough, there were old Italians at the bar, their eyes flicking over every person through the door, lingering on the young pretty women, the families with boy babies, scorning our queerness, even though we were open-hearted. The old Italians were loud as history, broken down, breaking down everyone around them. The sauce was not our mothers' red sauce, but we were reminded of our mothers, which made us soft with each other.

Why don't you clean anymore?

I clean.

You know what I mean. Remember when you called my mom crying that I never dusted the baseboards. How come you never dust the baseboards anymore?

I do other things.

But there were things you always did—the top of the refrigerator, descaling the coffee pot, changing all the filters . . . I loved it when I opened the door and the whole house smelled like lemon Pledge.

Go for it. Get down on your hands and knees and clean like a woman.

A weekend in New York City. We saw a Japanese play in translation and ate perfect Japanese food at a tiny Japanese restaurant. The next day we saw a musical, ate cannoli at Ferrara's, had dinner at Gramercy Tavern, and walked a hundred miles. Sunday we stood in line and ate brunch with all the East Village hipsters. To surprise me, you took me to Roosevelt Park where the old

Chinese men were out with their *hua mei*—Chinese songbirds in
bamboo cages. All around us birds singing.

What's wrong?
      Nothing.
      Something is clearly wrong. Why are you so bothered?
      I just want to be quiet.
      Are you pissed at me? What did I do?
      I'm not pissed.
      Just tell me.
      Okay. I feel like you don't respect my time. Or my priorities.
      *You've been here all morning! You don't know how to man-
age your time, you can't multitask, and your priorities change
like the wind. I never know what arbitrary boundary I'm vio-
lating. I never know when I'm going to make you mad.*
      You want to know when I'm mad? Now I'm mad.

On a dog walk in Warren Park in Chicago, he asked me about
regrets. I was old enough now that there were more years
behind me than ahead. "Is there a change you want to make?
Something you want to do?" I had seen a career counselor. I was
in the middle of applying for another advertising job. "I want to
go to graduate school," I said. "Let's make it happen," he said.
He read my application essays. We danced together at my graduation party.

Can you chop some carrots for the salad?
      I don't need a salad.

Not for you. It's for dinner and our guests

I bet nobody else needs a salad either. You don't need to make a salad for people who don't care.

I care.

About lettuce in a bowl?

I care because I'm cooking dinner and I want to cook what I want.

You'll be the only one who wants a salad.

The week in the cabin on Moose Lake. The osprey nests in the dead aspen trees, a prehistoric forest. The nightly tick check, dead ticks floating in a jar of rubbing alcohol. You were reading *Crime and Punishment*. We woke up before sunrise and ate ice cream from the carton. One spoon. *They were renewed by love.*

We were crowded during the pandemic in our little condo, the two of us, feeling cramped, the cemetery where we walked the dogs closed in the lockdown due to frequent burials. Over the summer we tried to find a house to rent outside of the city for the fall. We needed a change of view, we needed to stretch our legs, we needed the world to change. We wound up driving around within an hour of the city, checking out places and communities as best we could beyond the windshield of the car.

A friend asked me, Where are you now with Carl's transition? Which is to say, where was I now with life?

We moved to Rhode Island. I will miss Elizabeth Warren, Ed Markey, and Ayanna Pressley from Boston. My favorite things about Boston were the proximity to New York City and that Logan is a major airport—we could get to anywhere from Boston.

We live in a one-level house now, built in the sixties. The house is a square around an open interior courtyard. The courtyard is empty. We had heard from one of the previous owners, a gay hair stylist, that the parties hosted in the house were legendary. "That courtyard would be crowded with people who liked to get naked and lay in the sun." I look at pictures of courtyards with fountains and an olive tree, round wrought iron tables and terra-cotta wall planters. I think about naked bodies in our courtyard. Maybe ours. We don't know what the courtyard will be yet. We live around it, an empty, open space of uncertainty, a presence of possibility, like a marriage.

afterword

I'm not an especially astute or articulate observer of our political scene. Today, as I write these words, one month into Trump's second presidency, thousands of federal employees have been fired, our allies are turning away from us, social programs are being cut everywhere, scientific research has been censored, and more than seven hundred anti-trans bills have been introduced into legislation since the first of the year.

As each daily, nearly hourly attack against science, the environment, and arts and education is reported, as civil rights violations are posted, as our social protections and rights are dismantled, I tend to spin and fret: What to do, what to do? I feel provoked and overwhelmed, exhausted and rageful. Following the 2016 election, I hosted postcard writing parties from our dining room addressing our elected officials on matters we cared about. I'm a writer. I gravitate to the individual story, rather than the sweeping epic, the moment over the broad stroke of history. Every day since hearing that this book will be published, I've wondered if I shouldn't pull the manuscript. I'm a lesbian married to a trans man. The widespread and terrifying attacks against trans people make my personal concerns seem petty and self-indulgent. And there is something in this moment in time, in our collective history, that also feels familiar to me. The questions I have for myself as a writer are the same as the questions I have as the wife of a trans man, as the daughter of a second-generation Sicilian immigrant, as an older woman. How will we live now? As a writer I ask myself how to move forward and keep working with nuance and grace in personally and politically tumultuous times. I've circled around the preoccupations and obsessions—in books, film, music, art, and cultural history—that led to these essays, trying to reflect my own placement in and out of times of shifting social understanding. Each time I return to a particular obsession, the world has changed again: it is changed, it has changed, and I have changed in the act of returning.

March 2025
South Kingstown, RI

acknowledgments

More and more, I think it is a miracle that any book gets published these days. This is a work created from memory and judgment. I have recreated events and conversations imperfectly, with equal measures of bias and sensitivity, I hope.

Thank you to my generous and tolerant writing pals, who were with me every word of the way: Helen Fremont, Lenore Myka, Genanne Walsh, Tracy Winn, and Stan Yarbo. Thank you to my support squad, Barrie Jean Borich, Mary Cappello, and Jean Walton, for encouragement and friendship above and beyond the page. Thank you to my dearest Sujata Swaroop, whose couch and kindness supported me when I couldn't put one word in front of another. Thank you to heartfriends Nancy Allen, Caitlin Thornbrugh, Diane Johnson, Margaret Kellogg, Dianne Lee, Susan Simmons, and Judith Katz, who witnessed the origin of these essays and celebrated with me at the culmination of the book. Thank you to my forever Femme Sisters Cheryl Borden, Ann Freeman, and RoAnne Elliott. Thank you to the Warren Wilson Program for Writers, which remains my most steadfast community of encouragement and collegiality.

Time, space, and financial support are essential to the creative process. Thank you to the Vermont Studio Center, Nancy

Allen, and Diane Johnson and Margaret Kellogg for space and time to work on this collection.

Thank you to Geoff Kronik, my first friend in Boston, who taught me how to make curry, who shared his love of the sand-hill cranes with me, who should still be here.

Thank you to The Ohio State University Press, to David Lazar and Patrick Madden, to Charles Brock, who designed a cover that took my breath away, and to the brilliant staff of Mad Creek Books—Kristen Elias Rowley, Rebecca Bostock, Meghan Tarney, Samara Rafert, Olivia Sergent, Juliet Williams, Stuart Rodriguez, and Elizabeth Zaleski—who aren't just publishing a collection of essays but affirming the reality of trans and queer lives as a vital part of the American landscape.

notes

The following essays, or portions from them, first appeared elsewhere, sometimes in earlier forms:

"Men I Hate: The Stasi Men," *Guernica*, March 2, 2021. With thanks to Michele Moses.

"Becoming Queered" (as "First Home, Last Home"), in *Right Here, Right Now: The Buffalo Anthology*, edited by Jody K. Biehl (Cleveland, OH: Belt Publishing, 2016). With thanks to Jody Biehl.

For research and inspiration in certain essays, I drew on the following:

"changing the story"

This essay is framed by *Austerlitz* by W. G. Sebald.

"the man next door"

This essay is framed by the autobiographical novel *So Long, See You Tomorrow* by William Maxwell.

"becoming queered"

The Linda Ronstadt reviews come from Lester Bangs's "Linda Ronstadt Review," *Penthouse Magazine,* October 1972, and Stephen Holden's "Heart Like a Wheel," *Rolling Stone,* January 16, 1975. Information about Catherine Opie's photographs of Elizabeth Taylor's possessions is from https://museemagazine.com/culture/art-2/features/catherine-opie-home-invasion and https://www.artforum.com/features/star-turn-catherine-opies-elizabeth-taylor-photographs-218840/.

"cities and bodies in motion"

This essay is framed by *Invisible Cities* by Italo Calvino (translated by William Weaver). The "Possible City" subsection "Moving While Standing Still" is based on *This American Life* episode 162, June 23, 2000, "Moving: Sleeping in Mommy and Daddy's Room."

"the burning bed"

The epigraphs are excerpted from *Called Back: My Reply to Cancer, My Return to Life* by Mary Cappello (New York: Fordham University Press, 1921); *Nox* by Anne Carson (New York: New Directions, 2010), © 2010 by Anne Carson, reprinted by permission of New Directions Publishing; *Rage Becomes Her: The Power of Women's Anger* by Soraya Chemaly (New York: Atria, 2019); and "Cut" by Catherine Lacey, *The New Yorker,* April 15, 2019, © 2019 by Catherine Lacey, used by permission of the Wylie Agency. On current-day positive-thinking approaches to cancer, I quote Poorvi Mittal's "Cancer: Its Genesis and Cure," *LifePositive,* April 2004, https://www.lifepositive.com/cancer-its-genesis-and-cure/.

Information about Phineas Gage is from https://news.harvard.edu/gazette/story/2015/10/lessons-of-the-brain-the-phineas-gage-story/.

"the stasi men"

My Berlin book club read Anna Funder's *Stasiland: Stories from Behind the Berlin Wall* (London: Granta Books, 2011).

"men i love"

The epigraph is excerpted from "Ladies Room," in *57 Octaves Below Middle C,* © 2017 by Kevin McIlvoy, used with permission of Four Way Books, all rights reserved.

21ST CENTURY ESSAYS

David Lazar and Patrick Madden, Series Editors

This series from Mad Creek Books is a vehicle to discover, publish, and promote some of the most daring, ingenious, and artistic nonfiction. This is the first and only major series that announces its focus on the essay—a genre whose plasticity, timelessness, popularity, and centrality to nonfiction writing make it especially important in the field of nonfiction literature. In addition to publishing the most interesting and innovative books of essays by American writers, the series publishes extraordinary international essayists and reprint works by neglected or forgotten essayists, voices that deserve to be heard, revived, and reprised. The series is a major addition to the possibilities of contemporary literary nonfiction, focusing on that central, frequently chimerical, and invariably supple form: The Essay.

---

*Annual Gournay Prize winner

---

*Annual Gournay Prize winner